A Western Horseman Book

Colorado Springs, Colorado

BARREL RACING

By Sharon Camarillo

with Randy Witte

Photographs by Darrell Arnold

BARREL RACING

Published by
The Western Horseman Inc.

3850 North Nevada Ave.
Box 7980
Colorado Springs, CO 80933-7980

Design, Typography, and Production
Western Horseman
Colorado Springs, Colorado

Printing
Williams Printing Inc.
Colorado Springs, Colorado

Sixth Printing: July 1993

ISBN 0-911647-06-6

DEDICATION

To my greatest fans, my dad and mom, for their patience and
ever-lasting love . . . to my husband Leo, who has opened
doors of opportunity, and instilled in me that insatiable
desire to excel . . . to those special friends who, through
their supportive attitudes, constructive criticism, and
exchange of ideas, have shared in my dreams to make barrel
racing a respected professional sport.

ACKNOWLEDGEMENT

To Randy Witte, who has taken the interest to analyze and
understand the sport of barrel racing, and the makings of this
competitor. To him I offer a heart-felt thank you. My special
thanks also to Darrell Arnold, for sharing his time and talent in
producing the photographs for this book.

Sharon Camarillo

SHARON CAMARILLO

CONTENTS

1 INTRODUCTION

On becoming a winner: "If I can do it, anyone can do it," says Sharon Camarillo. "It's a matter of wanting something badly enough, and sticking to your goals."

After qualifying for four National Finals Rodeos, Sharon Camarillo is respected as a consistent winner in barrel racing. She is also a skilled rider and trainer who has the willingness and ability to help others find success in this popular event. Her instruction is two-fold: Sharon explains how to train a horse for barrel racing, and tells how a rider can keep the horse working and increase the odds of winning.

This book is her formula for success—a package of knowledge she has acquired over the last 20 years by riding a lot of horses, good and bad, while trying to get the most out of each one. She has read and studied, asked questions of other professionals in the horse industry, and gradually developed her own successful training and conditioning programs. Her horses stay fresh and willing.

"Let's face it," she says, "barrel racing can become pretty dull for a horse. It's not like working a cow, or roping. There are three stationary objects in the arena, and the horse can get sour running the same pattern. In order to avoid this resentment, I've learned to do a lot of training and conditioning away from the barrels."

Her winning edge comes from preparation—at home and during the warm-up period before a barrel run at a rodeo. In the text, she tells how to read a horse, to feel when he's warmed up sufficiently to deliver peak performance during a run for the money.

Sharon is also a former model who has been a trend-setter in fashionable rodeo clothing, something that goes back to the days of her youth when she felt determined to prove that women in rodeo can compete and still "look like ladies." But a good appearance is necessary to her for a couple of other important reasons.

"The crowd always likes to cheer for a fast horse or a pretty girl who looks flashy," she says. "When I select my barrel racing clothes, they won't be clothes I'll wear on the street or around home—they're costumes that show up well in the arena. Part of my responsibility as a professional barrel racer, I believe, is to dress for the crowd, to help give the people their money's worth; it's good for the event and it's good for the rodeo. I also know if I feel good about my appearance, naturally I have more confidence. It all ties in with winning."

Sharon also offers a bit of inspiration to every youngster who wants a horse but doesn't have one. She was raised on the edge of Los Angeles—not on a ranch—and her initial contact with the equine world came when she was a little girl on Redondo Beach. Sharon's father, Bob Meffan, took her to the pony rides there, and unknowingly provided her with the beginning of a lifetime interest in horses and riding. When Sharon was a teenager, dad took her to the National

Sharon and her barrel horse Seven, competing at Cheyenne, Wyo., in 1979.
Photo by Jan Spencer

Sharon Avril Meffan and one of her early mounts.

Finals Rodeo when it was held in L.A., never imagining that the contest would instill in her a goal to compete and win at rodeo. "If I can do it, anyone can do it," she states. "It's a matter of wanting something badly enough, and sticking to your goals."

Sharon's rodeo career began in earnest in intercollegiate competition at Pierce College in the San Fernando Valley. There she won the regional goat-tying and all-around titles, as well as a rodeo scholarship to California State Polytechnic, which fields some of the toughest rodeo teams in the nation.

Sharon went on to win the intercollegiate (NIRA) goat-tying championship in 1970, and the same year graduated with a bachelor's degree in business administration. That year she also realized in order to maintain a future in rodeo she would have to shift her interest from roping and goat tying to barrel racing and acquire a barrel racing horse that was competitive with those in pro rodeo. She joined the GRA (now WPRA), and began buying and training a succession of barrel horse prospects for her own use.

She worked as a flight attendant for Western Airlines over the next five years, training and competing on her days off. She won the 1974 WPRA steer undecorating title along the way, but barrel racing continued to be her prime interest.

Early on, she bought Rex, a hot-blooded gelding off the track, and from him learned that "speed isn't the only factor in making a good barrel horse. Rex could run, but didn't really like to turn." Still, she admits, he was a good step to her next horse, and her next . . . .

"Looking back," she says, "I think of the horses I've gone through, and sometimes wish I could start them over, applying some of the methods I've learned along the way. I think it would make a big difference in how the individuals turned out."

After she was married to Leo Camarillo, the venerable team roping champion, Sharon started working with her husband's calf horse, Charlie, who at the time was 14 years old. "He had been started on barrels in his youth," she says,

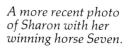

"and after Leo bragged on him long enough I took him to the arena to see what he could do." Charlie went on to win several local and state championships, was in the top 20 in WPRA competition, and is still running strong in collegiate competition, well into his 20s.

Of all the horses Sharon has worked with, a 15-3 hand, 1,250-pound Quarter Horse gelding she named Seven proved to be the greatest challenge to her training ability. In spite of his unusually volatile nature, Seven has been her best horse to date. With Seven's help, Sharon won the Sierra Circuit title in 1979, the same year she qualified for her first of four straight NFRs.

Sharon and Seven are still an explosive team with a very high win average, but she prefers to compete a little closer to home these days. Sharon doesn't thrive on travel the way Leo does, but when she goes, she goes to win—and usually does.

Randy Witte

2 GOALS

My goal with this book is to help others learn how to win and enjoy the competition at whatever level they choose.

Everyone needs a goal, something to work toward. When I started out to be a barrel racer, both my parents and the horse-oriented people I'd been raised around questioned my decision. I had grown up in the city, but had gained quite a bit of riding experience through summer and weekend outings, and at a family friend's stockyards. I loved to be around cattle and horses, but I also knew I didn't have the financial backing to get into showing horses.

About that time my Dad took me to the National Finals Rodeo in Los Angeles. I took an interest in the women's barrel racing. I could sense my adrenalin rush as the horse's hoofs pounded the arena dirt, and the crowd cheered. It was exciting to watch—pretty girls and fast horses. I began to wonder if there would be a chance to combine the skill and expertise of showing performance horses with the fast pace of barrel racing.

As I began to learn more about the sport, I knew I wanted to modify my original goal of just running around three barrels. I wanted to change other horsemen's attitudes about the sport. Not only did I want to be recognized as a competent barrel racer by my peers, but I also wanted to be recognized as a horsewoman outside of the rodeo business. At that time I hadn't seen that recognition given barrel racers. That became my goal. I began to watch, ask questions, experiment, fail, modify, succeed. To top it off, I not only wanted to

be recognized as a horsewoman, but as a lady as well. My ultimate goal was to ride well, and look good doing it.

Today I feel that same desire. I still ask questions and continue to look for better ways to work my horses. When I look good, when my horse looks good and is working well, I feel more aggressive and confident when I compete. While I was growing up I was lucky to have a mother who liked to sew for me. Today there are great western clothes on the market that are fun and flashy to wear.

My next goal was to become a consistent winner; and then to qualify for the National Finals Rodeo. One of the proudest moments of my life was riding in my first National Finals grand entry alongside my husband Leo.

It takes a lot of drive and determination to qualify for the Finals. To compete for a world championship requires the same drive and determination in double. It takes a great horse willing to give everything he has, it takes luck, and, perhaps most important, it takes a partner; a parent or husband who wants the championship as much as the rider.

I feel it's important to keep goals in perspective. If you go and win, it's great; if you go and lose, believe me it's not as

Preparing for a run at the 1980 National Finals Rodeo. **Photo by Ken Springer**

10

Women, especially, need to learn how to ride aggressively. Ask the horse for a movement, then be prepared to take it if it isn't given immediately.

much fun. My goal with this book is to help others learn how to win and enjoy the competition at whatever level of competition they choose, without experiencing so many of the unnecessary trials and errors I went through.

As for the future of barrel racing, it's unlimited. In pro rodeo, we are starting to receive prize money equal to that offered in the men's events. There are high stakes futurities for young horses and more channels for organized youth competition.

We have come a long way. Barrel racing began as a simple activity for women and children who accompanied their dads and husbands to jackpot ropings. After the men roped, the wives and daughters would jump on the rope horses and pull or guide them around a barrel pattern. There were no barrel racing saddles or other special items of

12

equipment; no special training was required or known. If a horse could really run, or liked to turn, he would probably win the race. At that stage, a horse didn't have to excel in both areas to be competitive.

In the latter 1950s there came along some women competitors like Sammy Thurman, who added some innovations to the event. She designed one of the first barrel racing saddles for commercial production, and at the same time began to hold organized barrel racing clinics throughout the country. Sammy went on to win the 1965 world championship, and I have to give her a lot of credit for her sacrifices and contributions in directing barrel racing toward the sport it is today.

As the sport becomes more and more technical, the heavy-handed "whip and spur" method is being replaced by educated horsemanship. Riders are modifying their styles and training techniques to create better, more consistent barrel horses that stay willing and enthusiastic for a longer period of time.

This is the method I use and teach. My program is designed to put a good foundation on a horse and at the same time train and educate the rider. This enables the equine athlete to acquire a background that will help him reach the height of his ability. This same background—a solid foundation—is something we can both draw from when trouble arises. And in case an individual horse goes through his training program and just doesn't like barrels—and I have seen a few like this—he will still be a nicely broke horse that can be used for something else. Nobody likes a spoiled, sour, uncontrollable horse, and that's what my training program is geared to prevent at all costs.

I emphasize horsemanship throughout the book. Consistency and intelligent handling remain the key to successful communication with your horse. I also stress the importance of aggressive riding. Most women by nature are not aggressive riders. To get aggressive they get mad first, and that's a bad combination in any sport. At my clinics, I try to teach students to be the aggressor when they first get on the horse. That doesn't mean to kick the horse in the belly and whip him on the butt; it means when I ask for a movement, I'm prepared to take it from the horse—if he understands what I want—if it's not given immediately and willingly.

So many times at rodeos or jackpots I've seen girls make a mistake during a run, then go out of the arena and say, "Oh, I wish I could make that run over again. I'm so mad!" Well, why didn't they call up that aggressiveness *before* they began the run? It's a matter of being aware of your attitude at all times when you're around a horse. When I'm on my horses, especially when they are in training, I'm aware of their movements and attitudes, and prepared at any time to make a correction, if necessary. That's what I mean by aggressive riding.

Consistency in action is important in making a finished product. You can't let a horse walk all over you one day and expect him to respect you the next. When a finished horse enters the arena for a competition run, I hope I've taught him to respect me enough to make a good run. Like any of us, horses may have off days when they don't put out 100 percent, but on any day they should be responsive and respectful.

Now it's time to get down to business. Look at the world standings, and year after year you will see a lot of the same names. Every few seasons, however, a new name appears and it's usually near the top. Most likely she's a new member with an outstanding horse. Their fresh enthusiasm, and natural competitiveness, is hard to beat, and that combination overcomes their lack of experience. Meanwhile, the rest of us just have to keep working at making that winner. So let's begin.

Consistency in action is important in making a finished product. You can't let a horse walk all over you one day and expect him to respect you the next.

3 PROSPECTS

Seven smiles for the camera. As a cutting horse prospect, he was a little too hot to handle. With training and patience—and luck—he turned into a winning barrel horse.

Most rodeo cowboys and cowgirls haven't been able to compete with the rest of the horse industry in selecting the potentially great, well-bred horses. Most of us have to be careful how much we spend for a horse, because there is still only so much prize money available for us to win and recoup our investments. Dollar-for-dollar, we can't compete with the performance horse trainers for their cowhorse prospects, and we can't compete with the race horse people for the top running-bred horses.

So, strictly as a matter of economics, the barrel racer may end up with another trainer's reject—a race horse that can't run fast enough; a cowhorse that's too hot; a reining horse that doesn't have the mind to be a futurity prospect. Sometimes it works out. A horse may not be suited for one event, but can go on to excel in another.

One thing all great horses have in common is *heart*—an attribute that cannot be spotted automatically in any prospect. Take the top 15 horses at the NFR, for example. They include big horses, small horses, nice-looking horses, and others that look a little coarse. But they all have one thing in common, and that's plenty of heart.

What we have to remember as we search for our ideal horse is that the quality of the individual is what's impor-

I prefer a nice-looking head on a horse, but pretty is as pretty does. I've seen beautiful athletes with coarse-looking heads. This is Chance, my latest trainee. Note the length of his neck and clean, fine throat latch, all of which adds balance and flexibility in the barrel racing athlete.

Size in a horse is irrelevant. What all great horses have in common is a lot of heart.

tant. It's true that a well-pedigreed horse will have better selling credentials, but the breeding alone offers no guarantee the individual will excel. Of full brothers or sisters, one may make it, the other may not.

What particular pedigrees do, however, is give us an insight into a horse's background. There are bloodlines that crop up in barrel racing circles more than others. They are lines that breed for the particular qualities that adapt a horse for our event. Barrel racing, for example, requires a quick, athletic horse that can run, but has the mind capable of keeping those volatile qualities under control.

I live in a pretty good part of the country as far as availability of horses goes. I may hear from a trainer that he has a futurity prospect that's athletic, but a little too hot on cattle. As far as I'm concerned, that's great—as long as the trainer hasn't confused "hot" with "crazy." The horse will have a good foundation on him, and I'll be able to adapt

him to the barrels with a little training. Since barrel futurities accept horses as four-year-olds, that's another plus in our favor. We may be able to pick up a horse that was shown in another futurity event as a three-year-old.

While we're on the subject of futurities, I'll have to say I've seen few good, young horses that excel at futurities and go on to make great open horses. I'm not sure why this is, but I have a theory that the young horse has been asked for so much so early that he or she doesn't have anything more to give. Lynn McKenzie's great horse Magnolia Missile is an excep-

Barrel racing requires a quick, athletic horse that can run, and has the mind capable of keeping those volatile qualities under control.

15

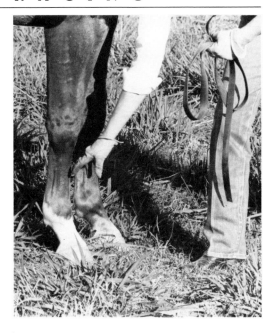

There should be good length between the cheek of the rump and hock; this length, combined with short cannon bones (top right), will help the horse travel close to the ground, giving him a balanced look and adding to that fluid "cutting horse style" I like to see in a barrel horse.

The horse's age is not all that important, unless he is to be a futurity prospect; an older horse may accept the pressures of training better than a very young horse.

tion. He was a futurity winner who went on to win two world championships for Lynn, and his career earnings are well over $300,000. He's one of the greatest barrel horses of all time, so what I'm saying is, there are always exceptions.

Before I buy a prospect, there are several things I look for. As I mentioned before, breeding will introduce me to what the individual has been bred to do; and his papers should help him sell in the future. The horse's age is not all that important, unless he is a futurity prospect; and as long as the horse's background can be accounted for, age may be in his favor. An older horse's mind will often accept the pressure you're about to apply easier than that of a young horse.

As for sex, I prefer geldings. Not only are they easier to haul, but their competitive moods are more consistent than those of mares or stallions. I'll have to say that I have been outrun by some outstanding mares and stallions, but for the most part, if the horse is to be used strictly for a rodeo horse, I don't feel you can beat a gelding.

Another important aspect in selecting a prospect is that the horse must want to be trained. Desire on the part of the horse will make up for a lack in the rider's ability or experience. However, sometimes this trait doesn't surface until the horse is into the training program.

As for conformation, I look for partic-

16

ular qualities in a barrel horse—low hocks and short cannon bones will allow this prospect to move close to the ground, producing that low, fluid "cutting horse" style I like to see in a barrel horse. I want the horse to have a long, slender neck, complemented by a clean throatlatch, with the head carried out and down to act as a body balancing pendulum. I not only look for a long underline, for the all-important stride, but I like to see a little extra length on the top line to give the horse the flexibility I ask for in my turns.

I want to see a long, sloping hip and shoulder for the pulling and pushing power he'll need to run and turn. I look for blemishes like splints, spavins, and windpuffs that may show weakness either in conformation or performance. The bone structure should be balanced to the size of the body in order to handle

Look for a long, sloping hip and shoulder for stride, speed, and the ever-important pulling and pushing power, necessary for performing fast, powerful turns.

The horse should have a long underline for stride, and I want to see a little extra length on the top line as well. This gives the horse flexibility in his turns. Bone structure should be in proportion to the size of the body in order to handle the strain of running and turning.

the strain the horse will be under; the hocks and knees should be large (box-like), and flat to help absorb concussion.

We can't ignore the feet. The old saying definitely stands, "No feet, no horse." I want good-sized feet with widely-set heels, all connecting to pasterns of good length and sloping proportionately to the line in the slope of the shoulder.

For aesthetic value and personal preference, I want a low tail set. This makes

a horse look like he's getting deeper into the ground than he really is. It's the style I want to see in my finished product.

As for the head, we can talk about the look in the eye, and the size and shape of the nose and nostrils, which enable the horse to suck in plenty of air, but the important part is that the head complements the body. Pretty is as pretty does, however, and I've seen some beautiful athletes with funny-looking heads.

The horse should be well-muscled in his hindquarters, showing plenty of muscle along the insides as well as outsides of his legs.

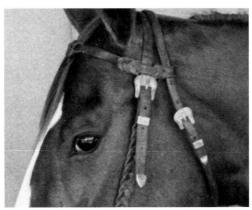

"Reading" the look in the horse's eye is a matter of personal interpretation.

Sometimes the shape adds to the character of the horse, and after you get acquainted, you wouldn't trade it for the prettiest of halter heads.

Like everything else about a winner, size is irrelevant. Theoretically, 15-1 to 15-3 hands is the size I like to look for. My horse Seven is every bit of 15-3, and I sometimes think that when running on hard or slick ground, his size may hinder him. On the other hand, when I get in heavy ground I appreciate his power. The rider should consider her size before she buys a prospect. I'm a fairly tall rider, and I'll choose a taller horse over a smaller one. I don't like to see a tiny rider overpowered by a disproportionately larger mount.

The bottom line, before I commit myself to buying, is how the horse handles himself under saddle. I'll choose one that likes to stop and turn over a horse that wants to run off. If the horse is green-broke, I'll watch his natural moves in a corral. I'll shoo the horse around and watch how he handles his body. I want to see his hocks well under him when he runs and rolls back; I want to see a free movement in his shoulders and hips; I want to see if he travels low and close to the ground, and if he uses his neck to balance himself.

After I finish studying his moves, I'll try to look into his eyes to see if he's had fun, and hasn't moved strictly out of fright. This is solely the buyer's gut feeling, but if there is still a decision to be made, then look in his eye. If you can read it, that may make up your mind.

Before we go on, I want to touch on one more point—buying a horse for a youngster. It's a mistake for a parent to buy a high-powered horse for a child to learn on. In order for the child to learn and communicate with a horse, he or she must first be given some confidence. Find a horse that has the intelligence to take care of an inexperienced rider. Introduce them to competition on their own level, and offer them the confidence that they can go fast without having a runaway. After the confidence builds, the rider will be ready for a little faster, more competitive horse.

Before I commit myself to buying, I want to see how the horse handles himself under saddle. I'll choose one that likes to stop and turn, over one that wants to run off.

The size of seat and cantle are irrelevant, as long as the saddle helps the individual rider ride the horse.

SADDLES

I endorse a saddle designed by modifying a Buster Welch tree. The ground seat is flatter than many saddles on the market, and this enables me to feel closer to my horse's back, and at the same time stay up and over my center of gravity. The saddle I use, on my big horse Seven, has a four-inch comfort cantle and fourteen-inch seat. Remember, though, that the dimensions of a saddle are as personal as buying boots. There are some horses that I prefer to ride with a 3½-inch cantle and a 13½-inch seat. As long as the saddle fits the horse properly, and at the same time sits the rider in the position she desires, the cantle and seat sizes are strictly a matter of preference.

The four-inch cantle helps me ride my big horse because he is very powerful and quick, and I feel I need all the help I can get riding him in order to not hinder his performance. However, when I ride a young horse, I usually select a lower cantle and a larger seat for more mobility in the saddle. When I get that horse to the point where he is ready for competition, I may change to a saddle that's more confining; one that will help me ride the horse more aggressively without worrying about staying in the saddle.

The fenders and stirrups are hung on my saddle so my feet and legs will hang directly under my hips. I don't want much play, forward or backward, in the saddle I compete in. This helps me to retain my body position during a run by

For barrel racing, higher swells and cantles help the rider "ride the horse"—not the saddle. The saddle on the left is the saddle I ride on Seven; to the right is the slightly smaller version.

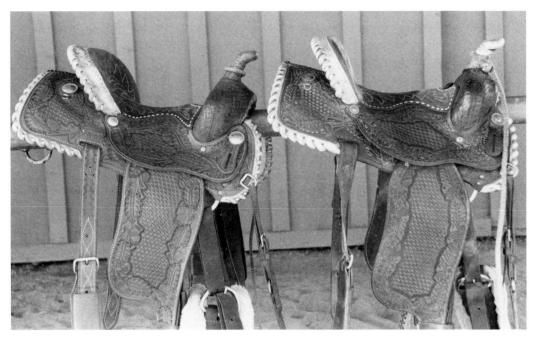

For balance, fenders and stirrups are hung on my saddle so my feet and legs are positioned directly under my hips.

not allowing my feet to get too far behind or too far in front of me. I don't want to rely on the horn to push or pull myself back into position. Just as I depend on the cantle to keep myself ahead of the horse, the swells of the saddle are also high enough to prevent me from leaning too far over the horse in a turn.

I prefer a square-skirted saddle. However, there is a weight factor involved when you consider the round skirt, or "speedster," compared to the square skirt. The choice is strictly a matter of preference.

I'm light, so I've never worried much about the weight of my saddle. However, I don't like it to exceed 32 pounds, including cinches and breast collar. I use a three-piece breast collar that snaps to the cinch on all my saddles; it helps keep them in position—they don't slip or roll. I use a back cinch, but since I don't really

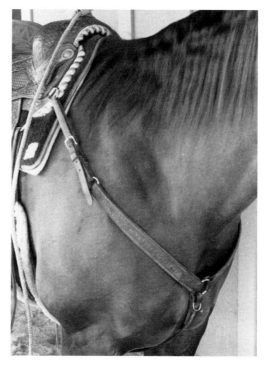

A three-piece breast collar is designed to help the saddle stay in position, and not roll on a horse.

21

I take pride in my equipment. A well-fitted saddle and pad complement the looks of any well-groomed horse.

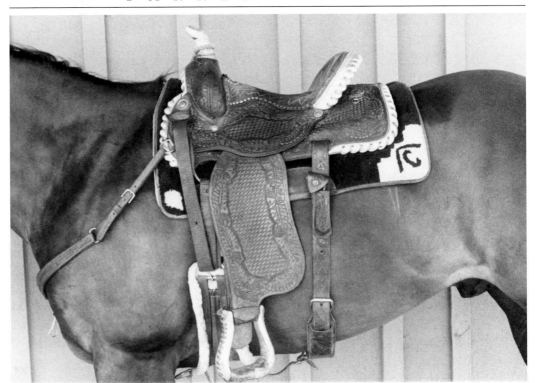

A saddle and latigoes should be kept in good repair. A clean, wide front cinch is important in well-fitted equipment.

snug it up, the only purpose it serves is as a visual aid in keeping track of my horse's weight. According to which hole I have to buckle, I can tell if he needs more riding or more feed. If the saddle fits the horse properly, it should stay in place with or without a back cinch.

My saddles are designed to fit down closely on a horse's back, both in front and behind. It's important that the bars on the back of the saddle are wide enough to allow this. I prefer one lightly-cushioned pad, and don't want to add more to compensate for a poorly fitting saddle.

When I pull off the saddle and pad, I check the horse's back to see if the pad has left even sweat marks. That's usually an indication of whether the saddle fits properly. If there are uneven sweating, sores, rubbed spots, or a place where the back is tender when it's brushed, chances are the saddle isn't fitting properly. A dirty pad is another cause for sore backs.

The "over-and-under" (the piece of nylon lariat attached to the saddle horn) hangs on the horn where it's handy but out of the way. It's important the saddle horn is neither too big or too small, so it will fit comfortably in the rider's hand.

Proper length of stirrups is important to a rider's balance. A good rule of thumb is to have two fingers between rider and saddle when standing up in stirrups.

Length of stirrups is a matter of preference. A rider may lengthen or shorten them to help her ride each individual horse.

A rider should not ride against the back of the cantle. The balanced position is obtained when the rider stands up in her stirrups, then sits straight down in a comfortable position, somewhere in the middle of the seat.

Saddle pads should be light and compact, and yet afford adequate protection to the horse's back. At left is a rug pad with removable felt liner; the padding on the right consists of a wool Navajo blanket with cool back lining. Blankets and pads should be kept clean to avoid soring a horse's back. The pad on the right does not set a good example for cleanliness!

If a saddle and pad fit properly, the horse's back will show no uneven areas of sweating. Dry spots are signs that a saddle is not fitting properly.

Raw spots or roughed hair are other signs of irritation caused by ill-fitting pads or saddles. A rider should check for signs like these, in the event that her horse isn't working up to his capability.

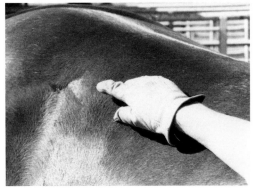

BRIDLES

There are primarily two training bridles I use—the ring snaffle and the English Springsteen. Each of these bits offer direct and lateral (sideways) contact with a horse's mouth. Most of the positioning and turning around barrels depends on this control.

I start every horse in a snaffle; when he's responding well to that, I'll put him in the Springsteen. I select a snaffle according to the individual. The twisted wire snaffle will lighten up a heavy horse. However, if the bit is too severe, and the corners of the horse's mouth become sore, I'll switch to a smooth-mouth snaffle.

I'll use a running martingale in conjunction with the ring snaffle. The adjustment is very important, and consideration must be taken to lengthen the rings so they will reach up to the point of the horse's shoulder. If the rings are adjusted too short, the horse's nose will be pulled down when he turns. He'll lead with his poll, and his weight will be shifted to his front end. All the martingale is designed to do is make up for the rider's inconsistent hands, and aid in setting the horse's head.

There's another rig I'll use with a snaffle bit, in place of the running martingale, for a horse who wants to carry his head low and his nose too far out. I'll make a "nerve line" or "poll martingale" with a piece of clothesline rope. I'll snap one end of the ring under the front cinch,

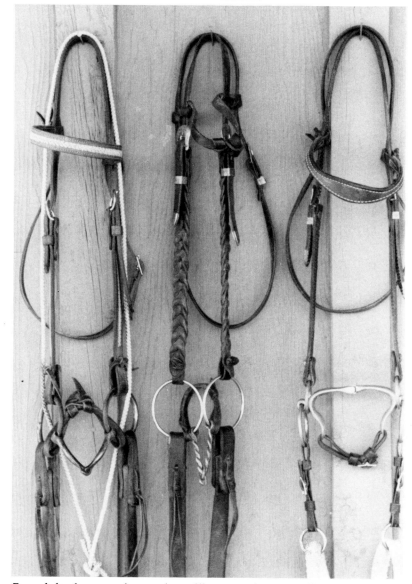

From left, the smooth-mouth snaffle, twisted wire snaffle, and Springsteen are bridled and ready for use.

Training snaffles are designed for teaching direct and indirect reining. I prefer heavy reins, preferably made of harness leather, for a good feel and good communication with the horse.

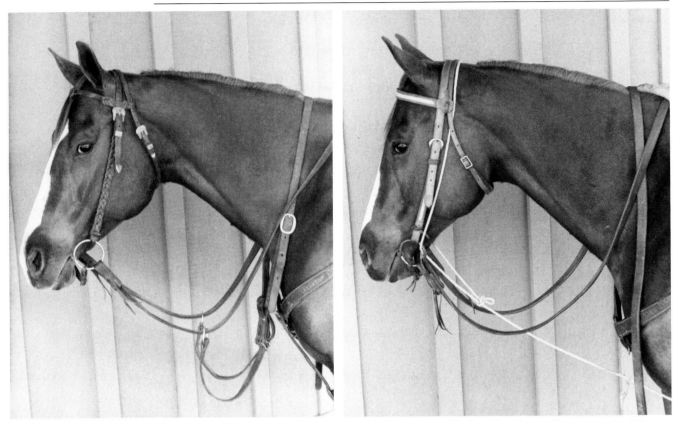

From left, a twisted wire snaffle fitted with martingale, and a smooth-mouth snaffle fitted with a poll-martingale. These training aids are interchangeable according to the needs of individual horses.

Riding with a poll martingale. This tucks a horse's nose and elevates his poll.

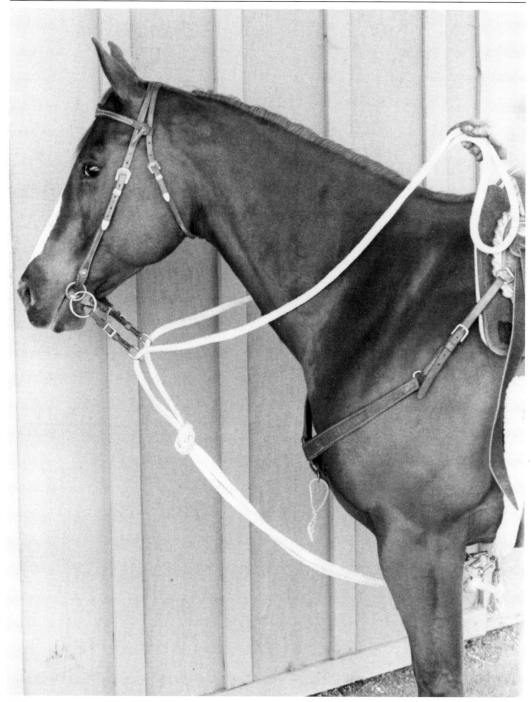

By first checking a horse up and letting him get used to the change in head gear, you'll eliminate the element of surprise that could be dangerous to horse and rider.

A Springsteen snaffle shown with a modified martingale. The knot below the bridle can be adjusted according to the amount of "draw" desired.

then bring the other end up through the ring of the snaffle, up over his poll, down through the other snaffle ring, and tie it in a bowline knot about a foot down from the horse's throatlatch. When a horse gets his nose too far out, he'll feel the pressure from the rope and bring it back into position himself, without the rider having to pull on him. This will also help a horse keep his nose tucked and poll elevated in his stops, enabling him to break in the loin, and keep his hindquarters well under himself.

I'll use this rig until I get good collection and a nice headset. It's similar to a tie-down in that it can be adjusted to varying degrees, according to what a horse needs. A word of caution: The rider needs to give a horse a chance to get the feel of a change in head-gear. By checking a horse up (chapter 5) and letting him get used to the change, you'll eliminate the element of surprise that could be dangerous to horse and rider.

A short-shanked curb bit. This is a nice transition bit—out of the snaffle and into the bridle. This can be used with a martingale and a four-rein set-up.

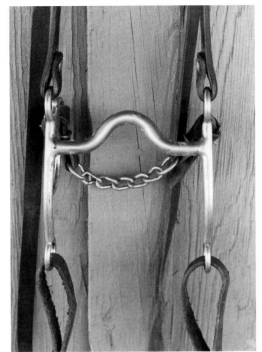

From left, an English polo bit, a gag bit with snaffle mouth piece, hackamore bit, and a Lynn McKenzie training bridle. I prefer the short-shanked version of the McKenzie bridle; it feels like a more balanced bridle to me.

Once a horse has progressed through the snaffle, to the point where he is responsive but ready for more speed and control, I'll switch to the Springsteen snaffle. This bit can be more severe than the ring snaffle, because the spoons give it more leverage. Because of similarities to a curb bit, the Springsteen is a good transition bit. During training, the Springsteen is rigged with draw-reins instead of the running martingale.

From the Springsteen, I'll usually select a gag bit with shanks and a curb strap, or a loose-sided bit with a curb or mullen mouthpiece. I prefer to use something that has slip in the shanks, because that's what produces the good, limber feel I want in a young horse. If these bits aren't giving me the control I want for a faster, competitive run, I'll try an English polo bit with a flat mouthpiece. A lot of competitors shy away from this type of

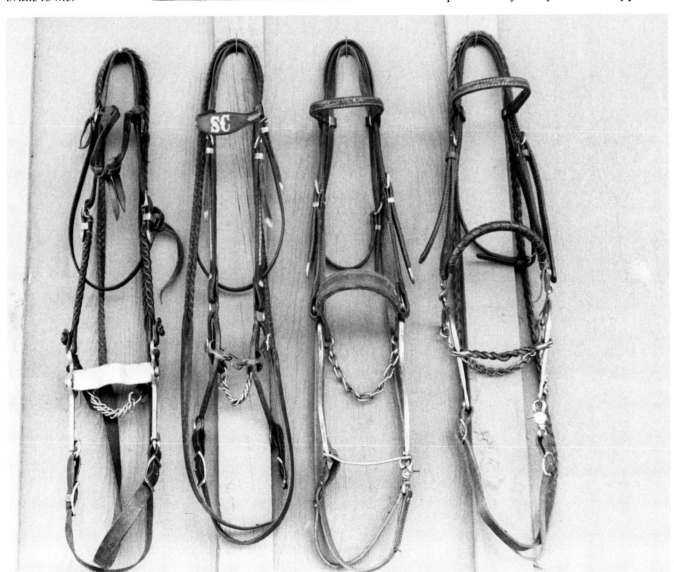

bit because it looks severe. I tried the bit in the first place because polo is similar to barrel racing as far as the horse's moves are concerned. The pelham version of this bit offers a place to add bit connectors. Each side works independently, so when I pick up one rein for a turn, I can really elevate a horse's inside shoulder—something that a solid-sided bit, like a curb, won't do.

A finished barrel horse needs two types of bridles. He needs a bit to be ridden in, exercised, conditioned, and tuned in, and he needs another bit for his competition runs. During the week, I may ride a horse in a gag, curb, or training snaffle, whichever complements him. When I run for the money, I put him in the bridle that gives me the control I need under pressure. I rarely work him in that bit, unless he needs his correction with speed; once he has been corrected, I'll take that bit off and save it for competition. When I put it back on him, I know he'll respond.

I get along well with the bits I've described because they fit my style of riding and training. The types of bits other barrel racers like vary according to their individual styles. Some riders run

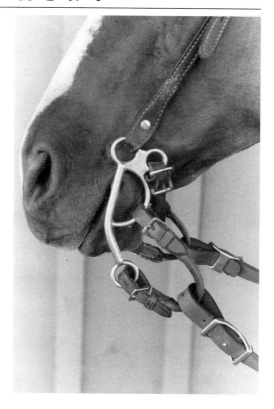

A pelham bridle with bit connectors.

Every horse, even a veteran like Seven, needs a second bit like one of the snaffles we've shown, for exercise, conditioning, and tuning.

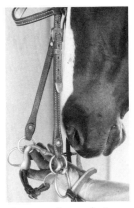

A young horse being bridled with a Springsteen. The snaffle should be adjusted so there is one wrinkle on each side of the horse's mouth.

straight to the point they want to rate a barrel, then guide the horse into the first part of the turn, set him into the ground, and roll him off his hocks. They can get by with a stiff-shanked bit. If I used the same bit, and tried to get the forward, lateral movements, which I'll describe in detail in the next chapter, my horse would probably fight it.

It's important that a rider understands how her bit works. That's one of the nice things about attending a barrel clinic. There's nothing more frustrating than to have a tack room full of bits, none of which seem to work on your horse. At most clinics, there will be a variety of bits on hand that you can try, and if one works then you can go out and buy it. It should be the responsibility of the rider to do some research as to exactly how the bit should be adjusted in the horse's mouth, and how it is designed to work.

A rider must also respect the control she is gaining over the horse with this equipment. Through patience and correct selection of head gear, a horse will learn he can't beat the bit, and he'll respond. It's important to note that control doesn't come strictly from head gear. Correct body positions, consistent cues

and leg aids all work together to make the horse and rider work as a team.

OTHER BITS

The Lynn McKenzie combination bit is one of the best correction bits I've found. I've experimented with this bit at my clinics, and found it to be a good bit for a lot of spoiled horses. Many girls go to a clinic and want instant results—they don't want to take the time to re-train. A lot of girls may have horses that are 14 or 15 years old; and how much change can we expect from these horses? You just have to try to find some little gimmick that will help cure existing problems. Lynn's bit has "whoa," elevation, and lateral control. But here again, a rider has to know how to adjust this bit. It's designed to fit high in the horse's mouth, with a couple of wrinkles on each side; the chin strap is very loose, and the bit works with a side pull effect. A lot of girls adjust it like a regular bit, with only one wrinkle on each side of the mouth, and with a fairly tight chin strap, but it isn't designed to work like that.

There are a couple more points on bits that need to be brought out. After

Control doesn't come strictly from head gear. Correct body positions, consistant cues and leg aids all work together to make horse and rider work as a team. Here's a slack run at a spring rodeo.

you've gone through your training snaffles and are looking for a good competition bit, but just can't seem to find one that feels good to the horse, have his teeth checked. Those three- and four-year-olds are losing teeth, and the bit may be bothering them. Maybe a horse needs to have his wolf teeth pulled. So, before the rider starts jerking on him, and becoming agitated, she should call the veterinarian for an examination.

Some horses may already have had their tongues cut by previous owners with bad hands who used bits that were too severe. This is another consideration. When you find a bit that works on a horse like that, set it aside. Save it for the competition.

A final thought on head gear: I don't rule out any bit or bridle, because horses are individuals. If it works, it's right. I never want a horse to learn he can get away from me. I won't sacrifice control for speed, so if I get to the point where I feel I am losing control, that's the time for me to make a bridle change.

"Neutral" adjustment for a tie-down can be seen when the strap comes tight as it is pressed against the horse's neck. From this point, it can be shortened or lengthened.

Three tie-downs: leather, rope, and chain.

TIE-DOWNS

A tie-down should complement the bit. It provides security and support for the horse in his turns and stops. A horse goes into a tie-down when he progresses past the ring snaffle and Springsteen bit. The tie-down takes the place of the martingale. I can ride a horse in the open without a tie-down, and that's fine. But for arena work, I use one of three types of tie-downs: soft leather, rope, or chain.

Sometimes I'll put a gag bit on a horse and he feels good, but I don't have enough rate. After checking the bit to make sure it is adjusted properly, I'll adjust or change my tie-down. The majority of horses will work better with a leather tie-down adjustment. You can tighten or loosen it, according to how the horse responds. A lot of horses like to run into the tie-down while they work, and as long as they come back to you when you ask for a check of gait or a turn, that's fine, too. If I have a horse that leans harder into the leather tie-down, I'll put on a rope or chain and let him lean into that a few times until he backs off.

Before you jump in, trying to change

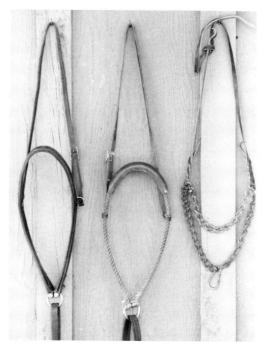

bits, which is one of the most frustrating aspects of trying to make a horse work, look at how the bit fits, analyze the horse's mouth, make sure the headstall and chin strap are both adjusted properly, then look at the tie-down. A tie-down can hinder or complement any bit, and the adjustment is as important as the fit of the bridle. If it's a leather tie-down, maybe it needs to be tightened up; if he doesn't respect that, go to the rope and tighten it up. If that doesn't work, go to the chain.

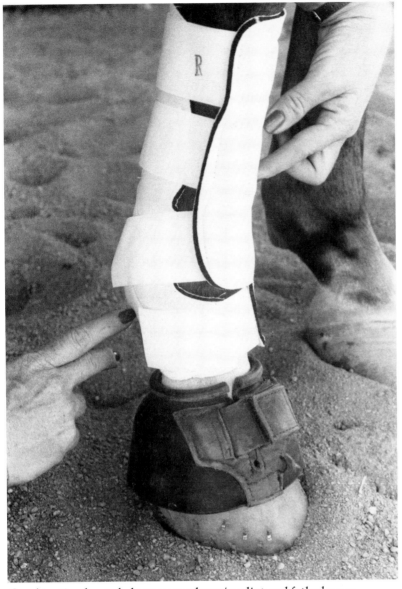

Combination boots help protect a horse's splint and fetlock area.

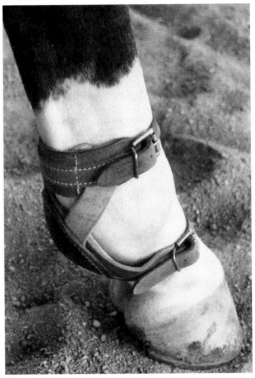

A bell boot split halfway down, and fastened with double velcro.

PROTECTIVE GEAR

I use three pieces of protective equipment: bell boots, combination boots (splint and rundown boots) for the front legs, and skid boots to protect the fetlocks on the back legs. This gear serves as preventive medicine; it helps guard against injuries. The front feet and legs need protection against overreaching, in which a hind foot over-extends and strikes a front foot while running or one front foot steps on the other in a turn. The hind fetlocks should be protected from rough ground in a stop.

Some horses may need additional protection. For example, a horse might get "speed cuts," caused by a front foot clipping on the inside of a back leg during a run. Another problem: hind legs may clip one another in a turn. But any time a horse is overreaching or clipping himself consistently, a horseshoer needs to be consulted, because there is usually an imbalance somewhere.

I stay away from the full velcro bell boots, because they seem to come off when they get wet, and that's when they're needed most—in mud, where a horse might slip and catch himself. I like a bell boot that's split halfway down, and then fastens with double velcro. Because the boot is partially split, it's easy to pull on over the foot, and easy to remove, but the double velcro keeps it on during a run. For a combination boot, I prefer the soft nylon varieties that have padded reinforcement in the fetlock and splint areas. If the horse doesn't have special problems behind, the standard roper neoprene skid boots are fine for the back legs, and that's what I use.

I don't use this protective gear when I just go for a ride. But if I'm going to work in the arena on a problem that will require speed, then I'll boot up. I'll also put boots on a young horse who doesn't know yet how to keep his feet under control, but it's rare for a young horse in training to need skid boots, because he's not going to be asked for stops at a high rate of speed.

ACCESSORIES

I carry an "over-and-under" on the saddle horn while riding my horses; and I usually have on spurs. I don't use spurs to make a horse run; I use a spur to make a horse move away from pressure. They're both aids, and it goes back to aggressive riding. First, I ask a horse to respond to my request. If he gives it, fine. If he doesn't, I take it. I'll lay a leg against the horse when I want him to move, and if he doesn't move, the spur is used to make him. If I feel I'm just irritating a horse with spurs, I'll take them off. You've got to know how to use spurs, and ride well enough not to be gouging the horse accidentally when he doesn't need it. Therefore, I don't recommend spurs—or a bat, for that matter—for an inexperienced rider, unless they are necessary to get some response out of the horse.

The over-and-under isn't as effective as a bat in some instances. A bat can be used more accurately to push a horse up into his turns. With the over-and-under, you have to reach down and find it first. But I'll sometimes use it, between barrels, and then again going to the finish line. The over-and-under also comes in handy if there's a problem getting a horse into the arena. It can be picked up to pop him, then dropped as the horse responds. One note: Lay the over-and-under across your leg before you make your run, and it will be out of the way but handy to grab when it's needed.

Laying the over-and-under across her leg before a run will help the rider know where it is when she needs it.

Spurs should be used by responsible riders who know where they are at all times. Downward sloping shanks help keep the spur out of the horse's sides, and are not as severe as the longer, straighter shanks.

5 BEGINNING BARREL HORSE

Foundation is the most important ingredient in the finished product.

When I talk about a beginning barrel horse, I mean a horse that is green to barrels. He might be a young horse or an older horse, but regardless of his age, he should be pretty well broke. By broke, obviously I mean I don't want him to buck or run off. I want him well introduced to the exercises that will follow. The exercises will make him supple, flexible, and, most important, responsive to leg pressure. He should be able to stop and roll back to some degree. He should change leads when I pick up the reins and bump him with an outside leg. And,

perhaps even more important, he should respond to direct and indirect reining. Regardless of the horse's age, I'll use the ring snaffle or Springsteen snaffle when I first ride him.

As the reader will learn, foundation is the most important ingredient in my finished product. I start a horse slow and continue to reinforce my training principles throughout the horse's education. I feel a horse taught with speed must be corrected with speed, and that's where you begin to have problems. With no solid foundation to draw from, how can

A young horse should respond to leg pressure, direct and indirect reining, before he is introduced to the barrels.

If a horse is green, or very stiff, start by first tying him to his tail. Caution should be taken to not tie him so tight that he can't get away from the pressure. Make sure the knot is secure, so it doesn't come loose. Then just let the horse "soak."

one possibly expect to keep a horse tuned and willing? My program is geared around time, and the fact I want my product to last.

I feel the more training I can do away from the barrels, the better. I teach necessary moves to a horse away from barrels, and then reinforce those movements on the barrels. I use the barrels for pattern work and tuning—at all times trying to avoid souring my horse.

CHECKING

One of the first things I do with a horse that wants to be heavy-mouthed, or resists when I ask for his nose, is to take him to a round corral, and check him back or around. I use split reins and a snaffle bit for these exercises.

Depending on how stiff the horse is, I'll check him to his tail or to the cantle of the saddle. I want to see him arc his entire body; however, I won't tie a horse so tightly that he's too uncomfortable. A "hole" must be left for the horse—once

1/ With a horse checked to the dee ring, after he's had time to soak, I move him forward with a slap.

2/ I'll use my other hand to slap his shoulder, moving his forequarters; don't let him pivot on his front end.

3/ As the saddle offsets, it indicates the horse has good bend from his neck through his back.

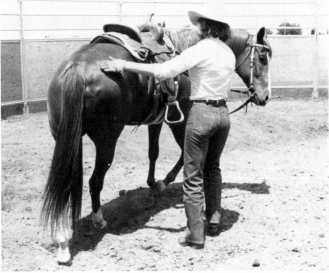

4/ Note how the inside hock reaches up and under the horse.

he responds he relieves the pressure from the bit.

Make sure the horse is in a safe pen for these exercises. Check for buckets he can step in or feeders hanging on the fence he can run into or rub against. From a short distance, keep an eye on the horse until you're sure he has accepted his circumstances.

As the horse relaxes, I'll go back into the pen and stand next to him, inside the arc. At this point I'll ask him to move around me. I'll simultaneously pat him on the shoulder and hindquarters. As he begins to move in the tight circle, I'm careful not to let him plant his front feet and swivel his hindquarters around, or pivot on his hindquarters. His circle should show forward movement as he

responds by walking in front and reaching up with his inside hind leg, crossing it over the outside hind leg. This exercise will teach the horse to limber up his shoulders, hips, and nose. This is the same forward movement I ask a horse for as he turns a barrel.

During the next few days I'll alternate directions with the exercise; however, I won't dwell on the checking, and will continue with his riding schedule. A little checking goes a long way. After three or four days of 10- to 25-minute sessions, depending on how well he responds, I'll discontinue the exercise, resuming it a few days later only if the horse isn't responding by bending and flexing in his turns.

Sometimes an older, seasoned horse

will get a little stiff in one direction or another. A session or two with his head tied around to the saddle horn may correct this. The pull from the saddle horn in comparison to that of the cantle is more similar to that of the rider's pull. The old veteran already should know the play, and this should aid in lightening him up.

If you come across a horse that is heavy in the bit, you might consider checking him straight back with the reins tied behind the cantle. This will make his mouth a little tender, and therefore lighter to the touch. For a real heavy-mouthed son-of-a-gun who is not willing to respond to "reason," take the split reins out of the martingale rings, bring them down between his front legs, back up and over the top of the saddle, and tie them together. Let him walk around with his head down for awhile. This should lighten up even the most heavy-mouthed horse. Consideration should be taken here, however, to determine if the problem is with the horse or the rider. Light hands make a light, responsive horse.

To resolve a similar problem in a young horse, bridle him without the reins attached to the bridle, and let him eat, drink and carry the bit for a couple of hours. This will aid in lightening up the horse, and at the same time teach him to carry and accept the bit.

Another time I call upon this exercise is when I change a bit on a horse. I'll check him straight back for a few minutes, and give him the chance to get the feel of the bit before I ride him.

It's important to remember these exercises are designed as *lessons, not punishment.* They must not be overdone, and should be well supervised by an experienced trainer. If the horse is checked too tightly, it could destroy his incentive to respond, because he can find no relief, whatever he does. If overdone, the exercises could possibly allow a horse to become too limber, or to find his own, unacceptable way to get away from the bit pressure. Hot-blooded, somewhat soured barrel horses can be pretty volatile at times, so utilize the exercise, then allow the horse to figure it out for himself before you ask for additional movements. This "soaking" time allows the horse to resolve part of the problem on

If a horse is "heavy" in the mouth, check him straight back to the cantle.

Run the reins between the front legs and tie over the top of the saddle.

Let him soak . . . This can be a real "attitude adjuster."

A seasoned horse may be lightened up by checking to the saddle horn.

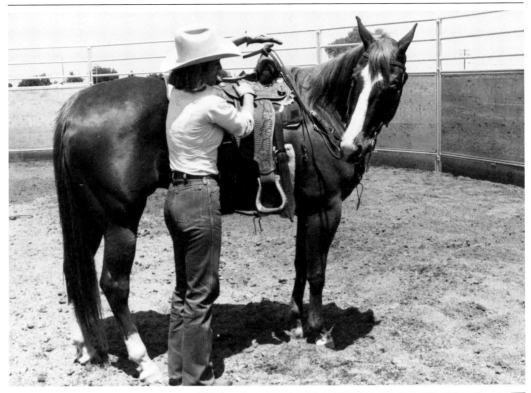

I'll introduce a new bridle by checking a horse up before I ride him. As he gives to the bridle, his poll will flex and his nose will tuck.

his own without additional resentment towards the rider.

PATTERNS

I use a variety of riding patterns to help condition and train a horse for barrel racing, and to keep him limber throughout his body. Some of these patterns are used only during the early stages of training, but others can be relied upon to help tune a solid, seasoned horse. A horse that can perform these exercises reasonably well will have a foundation that can be called up at any time in the future, should some kind of a problem develop.

For the majority of these exercises, you should be riding with some type of training bridle, like a Springsteen or ring snaffle. This will give you the direct and lateral control necessary to school the horse. Make sure there is plenty of room between your left and right hands, so one rein doesn't interfere with the other.

Don't attempt to do all these exercises every day—it's too much to ask of the horse, and nothing kills a horse's desire like fatigue. For example, too many lead changes, roll-backs, and limbering exercises, and a horse gets resentful instead of responsive. He'll try to figure out how to cheat the rider.

It's the responsibility of the rider to be in communication with the horse to see what he needs. I believe a horse can learn for a short period of time—maybe only 15 minutes of concentrated work—and that's about it for one session. Some horses can take more, some can't take as much. So again, it's up to the rider to watch and learn from the horse's responses. Something else to keep in mind—a horse can get sour from working too much on something he already does well. For example, if a colt really does a particular movement well to the right, but is not as smooth to the left, don't work as much on the right as you do on the left. I will touch up on some-

thing he does well from time to time, though, just to make sure he hasn't forgotten, and to give myself confidence that he has it.

Pattern A
THE CORKSCREW

This is probably the most important exercise I use through every phase of a horse's training and career. It's good to use on a "baby," one just starting out, for a high-strung horse that needs to calm down, and for an old horse to keep him supple and limber. I saddle up and walk the horse from the barn to the arena, then pick a nice big circle, at least half

To introduce these exercises, you should be riding in some type of training bridle. Then warm up the horse at a lope in a large circle, until he comes back to you, before you ask him for anything.

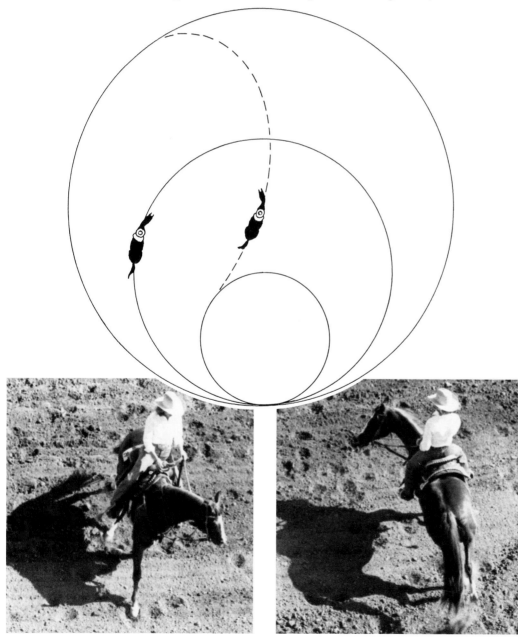

With the nose to the inside, during the corkscrew pattern, I'll ask the horse for smaller and smaller circles, until he has to break to a trot, before sending him back into a big circle in the opposite lead.

Make sure you leave plenty of room between your hands, so one hand won't interfere with the other while reining.

the size of the arena, and put him into a lope in the correct lead. If the horse is feeling fresh and high, and acts like he really wants to run, I just guide him around in that big circle. I don't fight him to slow down, I don't snatch at his face, I just guide him in that circle until he takes a breath and relaxes, and then I ask him to come back to me. At that point, I start into my corkscrew pattern. We make smaller and smaller circles. I reinforce the same body position I use in my barrel turns. I've got my weight in the stirrups with a little more pressure in my outside stirrup, and with my inside leg against his side. In other words, if I circle to the right, the horse is in the right lead, and I stand with a bit more pressure in the left stirrup. I have my right leg ready to bump the horse on the inside to hold the correct arc, which in this case would be the right arc. I'll continue to use a little nose pressure.

With this outside body position, I continue to screw him right down into a tiny circle, until he breaks into a trot. At this point, I don't relieve any pressure; I just let him trot or walk around in that little circle. This movement reinforces the idea that he has to give his nose to me, and it frees up his body from his hindquarters through his back to his shoulders. When the horse relaxes and gives me what I want—the same movement we worked on in the corral when we checked him around in that arc, I release the pressure, then pop him out of the circle in the opposite lead, and go back into the big circle in the opposite direction.

This exercise helps a horse with his leads, reinforces his body suppleness, and helps him work off his hocks—all the movements he will need when he runs barrels. The exercise also helps condition a horse. You'll be surprised how even the highest, craziest horse, once he's done this corkscrew—maybe twice in one direction and once in the other—will be ready to do something for you. It's a great warm-up.

Rider's hands (above) are in the "neutral" position—reins are short enough to offer leverage to reinforce cues. Be sure to use a secure, yet sensitive, grip on the reins (right).

Caution should be taken to not separate reins (left), or ride with reins that are too long, or with hands held too closely together. These are common mistakes riders make using split reins.

41

Pattern B
TWO-TRACKING

I like to teach a horse how to carry an arc while traveling in a straight line. I go into an alleyway that's maybe 15 or 20 feet wide, and work off one of the fences. If I use the left fence, I take the horse's nose to the right, using a direct rein, and we'll walk with the hip and shoulder parallel to the fence. His right front and hind feet will overlap each other as we move down the fence at a walk first, then a trot, and when the horse becomes familiar with the exercise, a lope. When we get to the end of the alleyway, I let him have his nose back, we drop to a walk, and I make a small half-circle and go back down the same fence. This time, we'll carry the opposite arc. The horse will reach up and across with the inside hock. This is the basic forward movement used in approaching a barrel and maintaining a pocket.

This movement also leads into the two-track. I'll zig-zag a horse; he'll travel diagonally while retaining a forward motion. I'll two-track to the right for 20 feet, then allow the horse to travel

Advancing in a forward arc, hip and shoulder should be held parallel to the fence.

A forward, diagonal movement is required for two-tracking.

42

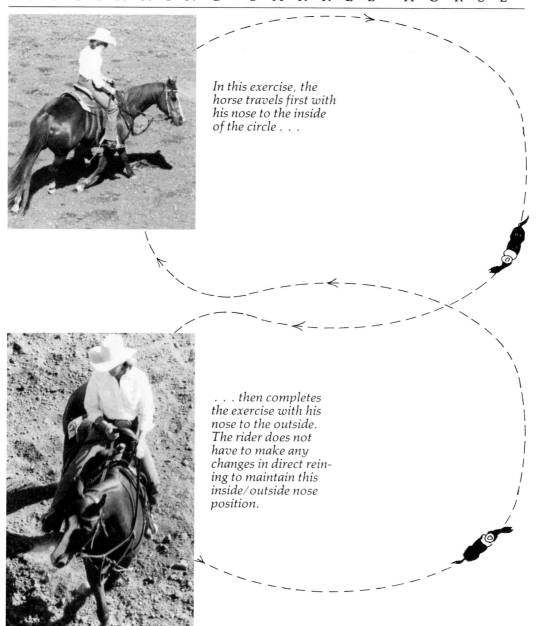

In this exercise, the horse travels first with his nose to the inside of the circle . . .

. . . then completes the exercise with his nose to the outside. The rider does not have to make any changes in direct reining to maintain this inside/outside nose position.

By tipping the horse's nose to the inside of the circle, the rider should be aware that the horse's shoulder is elevated and to the outside of the circle. Conversely, when the nose is tipped to the outside of the circle, the shoulder is forced to the inside. Remember—the horse should move away from leg pressure.

straight forward for 20 feet, then two-track for another 20 feet moving diagonally to the left. As this exercise becomes easy for the horse, you may ask him to two-track diagonally across the entire arena, utilizing both arcs.

Pattern C
A DIFFERENT FIGURE EIGHT

Picture two circles, touching, in the form of a fat, round, figure eight. The circles are probably about 30 feet in diameter, and I start one circle at a jog (collected trot), and use a direct rein on my training bridle. I will use little, if any,

inside or outside leg pressure—I'm sitting down in the saddle at a collected trot—and once again don't use any outside rein; I just hold the outside rein out of the way. The horse's nose is crimped to the inside of the circle, and I'm concentrating on pushing him forward, making sure the inside hock is starting to cross to the outside.

I complete the circle and go into the figure eight. But, I don't release the pressure on his nose. His nose will still be crimped, but it will be crimped to the outside of this circle, and the hock will cross over into the inside. Once again, what this does is limbers up a horse from nose to neck and shoulders, and most important, it limbers the back through

43

the hindquarters. This is a good exercise to help take out stiffness or tenseness in a horse.

Note: The first time you do this exercise, you might have to work on the exercise anywhere from 10 to 20 minutes, and the horse might be in a lather. The theory must be accomplished, to some degree, the first day . . . at least to the extent that the horse is beginning to understand the maneuver. A foundation is being laid for the next session. The important movement here is the forward/lateral motion in the hocks.

After I get a fairly soft feel in one direction, then I work him in the opposite direction, with the nose bent the other way. When the horse accepts this exercise, he is ready for Pattern D. But if it's the first day for Pattern C, the horse will probably be ready to call it a day. I'll make sure he is cooled down before I put him up.

Even at a standstill, flexibility, both laterally and vertically, is a very important asset in making a supple horse. Use a little bit of pressure on the reins in the direction you want the horse's nose to take—don't ask for it all at once—and over a period of time, the horse should give his nose willingly, to any degree, that the rider asks.

44

I lope in the correct lead, according to the direction of the circle, regardless of whether I have the horse's nose tipped to the inside or the outside.

Pattern D
NOSE IN/NOSE OUT

There's a nose-inside/nose-outside exercise designed for stiff horses who drop their shoulders and resist giving their noses. It's done at a lope. I pick up a circle, say in the left lead, left circle. It's a collected lope, but I have more than just a tip on his nose—it's a good gathering, and I'll hold him in that circle until he begins to relax and limber his shoulder.

Then I continue in that same circle, but take his nose to the outside—again using the outside rein—and lope for two or three strides with his shoulder dropped into the circle. Then I gradually take his nose back to the inside, pushing his shoulder once again to the outside. I use the nose to the outside at a ratio of about four to one. In other words, the horse takes about 20 strides with his nose to the inside, shoulder to the outside, to every five strides with his nose to the outside, shoulder inside. His shoulder begins to feel flexible. Remember to lope in the same lead whether the nose is to the outside or inside.

At this point, I may incorporate some lead changes—I'll stop, take a couple steps sideways, toward the middle of the circle, and ask for my opposite lead, and work the exercise in the opposite direction. As the horse relaxes and accepts the exercise, I'll add one more movement.

When the nose is tipped to the inside of the circle, the shoulder will be forced to the outside.

The position of the rider's hand will elevate the horse's shoulder. Raise the inside hand high along the horse's neck to regulate the shoulder elevation.

I'll have the nose to the inside, and I'll just raise my inside hand up along the horse's neck and ask him to hold the lead, but move outside the circle for three or four strides. Then I'll lower my hand and bring him back into the circle. This is the same movement you ask for when you create a pocket on approach to a barrel.

Almost every one of these exercises applies to the barrel race, and once you take a young horse off these exercises and put him on the barrels, he'll be loping through the pattern in no time at all. When you pick up an inside rein, he'll know to arc and move out, and when you drop a leg against him, he'll know to move away from the pressure. A lot of problems will be avoided entirely.

Note also: Raising the inside rein, and keeping his nose turned to the inside, will elevate a dropped shoulder. This movement can be added to any circle in which a horse wants to drop his shoulder, including a barrel turn.

BACKING

Another important exercise that should be used throughout a horse's career is backing. I see so many girls who back three steps and stop. And if they were to ask for a fourth step, they might as well be pulling on a brick wall. So I take three steps, four steps, maybe more. If the first two are easy for him and the third one is hard—he balks—I'll lighten him up and back him through that point where he wants to stop. When I back, I back until I want to quit, not until the horse wants to quit. I like a horse to move as freely going backward as he does going forward. I'll back straight, but I'll also incorporate some backing in a circle. When I ask a horse to back, I shift my weight back towards the cantle and pull the reins in a solid fashion. If he balks, I pull harder, instantly relaxing the pressure as he responds.

Backing . . . and backing in an arc (below).

When I ask a horse to back, I shift my weight back towards the cantle and pull the reins in a solid fashion.

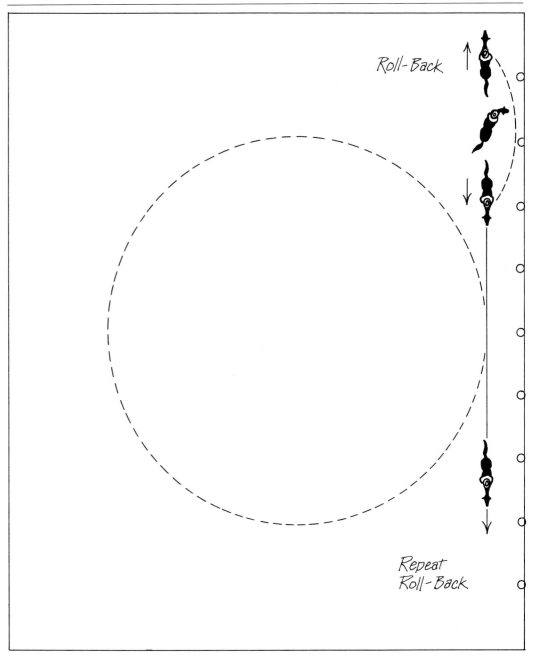

Roll-Back

Repeat Roll-Back

Circling the horse in between stops and roll-backs helps to keep him calm.

STOPS AND ROLL-BACKS

If I've got a horse that needs work on stopping, I'll use the fence as an aid. I'll pick the back half of the arena, where I've got two corners. There I'll lope the horse in a large circle until he is nice and relaxed. At that time I turn up the fence and lope toward the back end. About five strides before we get to the corner, I cue him for the stop by sitting down in the saddle, saying whoa, and drawing up on the reins. If the horse tries to stop on his own, I'll roll him back into the fence and lope to the other end of the

arena before asking him for another stop. If he bounces out of the stop, I will back him a few steps before I ask for the roll-back.

Here's where I modify the exercise to help a horse rate his barrels. After the horse has learned to stop straight, I ask for a slight arc in the horse's body as he is stopping. I use a little inside rein and outside leg pressure. This arc will help him drive the inside hock deeper up in the stop and turn. This is the position I will request as I rate and turn a barrel.

If a young horse is working at stopping, but is a little insecure, I won't pressure him too much at first. After two or three stops, if I feel he is at least thinking

1/ *After stopping, back the horse onto his pivot hock.*

2/ *Use a direct rein . . .*

3/ *Some indirect rein and outside leg . . .*

4/ *. . . to send him back in the opposite direction.*

about getting into the ground, that's enough. I'll take a fresh start the next day.

Once a horse begins stopping using the fence as an aid, I'll ask for a stop halfway down the fence. This gives the horse confidence that he can stop in the open.

To complete a roll-back, after the horse has come to a stop, I'll direct rein the nose into the side fence. As he starts into the turn, I'll release some of the nose pressure and lay the outside rein and my outside leg against him to push him off his hocks and out of the roll-back. The horse's weight has already been shifted to the hindquarters from the stop, and

the fence will act as an aid to keep him there, forcing him to pivot on his hind legs. As with any exercise, the horse must be shown how it is executed at a slow rate of speed, so he can learn the execution. After the roll-back has been completed, if the horse is high, I'll circle until he calms down.

As the horse calms, I'll take him out of the circle and back up the opposite fence. The roll-back exercise is great for teaching a horse how to collect himself in order to turn and drive away from a barrel. It's important to make the roll-back a smooth, continuous motion, without hesitation, as the horse sets, turns, and leaves in the opposite direc-

As a horse advances, the rider should be sure to stay ahead of the motion (top) as she sends her horse back down the fence (below).

You can always use a fence as an aid in roll-backs.

None of the exercises will be learned by a horse overnight. A horse's education comes from patience and awareness on the part of the rider.

tion. As I introduce the stop and roll-back exercise, I won't give much consideration to leads; however, later on in the schooling, the horse should break out of the roll-back in the correct lead for the circle he's headed into.

As the horse begins to respond to my cues, he may begin to anticipate the stop before he gets to the end of the fence. I'll push him up into the stop for the turn, then ask him to roll back again into the side fence. If a horse stops nicely and really gets into the ground at that point, I'll stand and let him catch his breath before calling it a day.

As the horse advances from dependencies on aids, I'll progress to loping circles in the arena, pick up an outside rein without setting up the horse in a stop, roll back to the outside of the circle, and go the other direction in the opposite lead. This helps teach a horse that when I pick up the reins, he'd better be looking for some ground to get into. It helps teach him to stay on his hocks in a tight turn, and to push off his hocks when he changes direction. If I feel the horse still needs an aid, I can move my circle over so it's close to a side fence. Here I can use the fence for rate, and roll back into the open.

'NO STOP/NO START'

Each of these exercises can lead from one to another. To use the word "stop" in

another context, I want to say that I like a "no stop/no start" when I'm working a horse on these exercises. The horse won't anticipate what may be coming next. Unless I'm rewarding a horse for a particularly nice move, I generally don't complete one exercise, then stop, or quit, and walk to another part of the arena to start on another exercise. If I roll back into the fence, I'm going in the opposite direction, and can either practice another stop and roll-back, or just turn into a circle to set up another exercise.

All of the exercises are compatible; I can go from one to another in any se-

50

quence I choose, and unless previously designated, at any gait I choose. Just a reminder—caution should be taken not to over-drill or fatigue the horse while he's in training. Most likely, if a horse gets too tired, the session will end in frustration for both horse and rider.

Remember that a horse has a fairly short attention span. Even though a riding session may last for an hour, ten to fifteen minutes of concentrated training should be enough for each exercise.

I'll pick up an outside rein, roll to the outside of the circle, and travel in the other direction in the opposite lead.

Rewarding the horse is an important part of training. At the end of a training session on barrels, I'll often walk to the first barrel, dismount and loosen the cinch (left). This gives the horse a chance to relax in the proximity of barrels. A gentle pat and rub on Chance (right) tells him I was pleased.

51

6 NOW FOR THE BARRELS

1/ To begin, walk through the pattern, then jog through it. Head fairly straight to that first barrel.

After a horse is doing well on the exercises we covered in the previous chapter, he's ready for the beginning barrel pattern. Walk the horse through the cloverleaf once of twice, just to show him what the barrels are. Then jog him through the pattern, guiding him around each turn. He's basically broke; you've used direct and indirect rein on him, direct and indirect leg pressure, he can pick up both leads, stop when you want him to. He may not be great in any one area, but he's coming along.

Initially, I'll head fairly straight to the first barrel at a slow jog. At first I won't ask for much rate, because we're already traveling slow; rate (adjusting stride to turn), isn't important until you start to

2/ and 3/ (left and right). Ask the horse for arc by shifting weight to the outside, picking up the inside rein, and applying pressure with the inside leg. It's important to establish plenty of pocket as you approach the barrel. Cones were set up to help show the shape of the pocket. This isn't an exact measurement—the size of pocket will vary from horse to horse—but the cones illustrate the average shape of a pocket, and the distance between horse and barrel.

52

build speed. So we'll jog up to the barrel, remembering to build plenty of pocket. We'll come out close on the back side and head straight across to the second barrel. It'll look like we're going to run into that second barrel, but when we get about ten feet from it, I'll pick up on the left rein (providing we started with a right barrel first), apply pressure with my left leg, shift my weight to the outside stirrup, and he'll begin to form a pocket. At that point, his body will move around the barrel, and his nose will be to the inside of the circle. He'll come out of the turn, close to the barrel, and we'll head straight for that third barrel. Again, I'll pick up the inside rein, apply left leg pressure, stand to the outside, and make him arc around the barrel. He'll show a nice, free, forward movement behind. He's literally beginning to reach up with that inside hock.

I never work a horse at a trot, jog, or lope, from the third barrel straight back to the finish line. I don't want the horse to anticipate and consequently "bow off" the last turn. Instead, I'll make a complete turn around the third barrel and head toward the side fence, then go

6/ Complete the turn close to the barrel and head straight for barrel number two.

4/ At a walk, the horse is bending nicely around the barrel.

5/ Notice how the right hind foot reaches up and over the left hind foot, and how the horse holds a proper arc.

Beginning Barrel Pattern

Leads are an important factor in helping a horse make a smooth run. Beginning at a lope, I remember to have the horse on his correct lead. Immediately after turning the first barrel, I will "drop him down" (from a lope to a trot), and this helps him change leads for the next turn. This early maneuver will give the rider more time to ride into position for the next turn. With proper training, the horse becomes seasoned; his lead changes should become automatic.

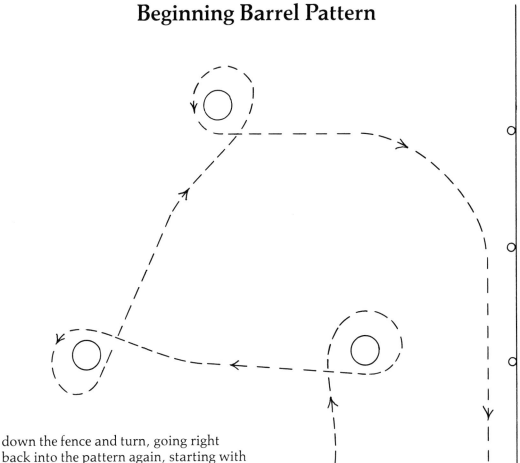

down the fence and turn, going right back into the pattern again, starting with the first barrel . . . no stop/no start.

Initially, to start a green horse, I'll go around the barrels like this eight to ten times a day, and I'll vary the pattern. I may go around all three barrels once, then go around just the first and second barrels, or first and third barrels, again using the no stop/no start program. I'll take him off one barrel and head straight for another, forming a good pocket for each turn. At this point I want the horse to relate: barrels equal turns—no matter in what order.

After the horse begins to watch the barrels, I won't work them every day. I might work them one day, then trail ride the next, or work on conditioning, and bring him back and trot around the barrels before I put him up. The following day I might go back to the arena and work on some of the exercises, then trot him around the barrels a few times before I put him up. The barrels will begin to be just another exercise for the horse.

The main thing to remember is that you don't want to over-work the barrels. The horse will get tired, bored, and soured. Once that happens, a horse's attitude is hard to readjust.

BODY POSITIONS

Even while working at a trot, I want to be aware of my body positions in the saddle. I start the horse's turns with the direct inside rein, and when I get to the backside of the barrel, I'll let off a little pressure on the direct inside rein and reapply pressure to the outside rein, reinforcing the movement with my weight to the outside stirrup. At the same time, I'll "scissor" my legs as I twist up out of the saddle to look directly at my next barrel. This body movement helps add snap to a turn. This is the beginning procedure, and what you want to work for is to be able to use direct rein all the way around the barrels, without having to reinforce the movement with much outside rein.

For proper balance in barrel racing, or any speed event, it's important that the rider's feet remain flat in the stirrup, parallel to the ground. The rider's weight

Feet should remain flat in the stirrup, parallel to the ground. the rider's heel and toe should also be parallel to the horse.

After completing the turn around the third barrel, angle off toward the side fence.

Something else for the rider to practice while working slowly—look to the next barrel before a turn is completed. This will help reinforce the rider's body position.

Remember, even while working slowly, to shift your weight slightly to the outside stirrup while turning.

1/ Going to the second barrel.

2/ Ride straight to the barrel.

3/ When you're about ten feet from the barrel, ask the horse for that forward, lateral movement.

4/ Allow plenty of pocket in order to give the horse enough room to turn.

5/ *Working at a jog. . . .*

6/

7/

Don't over-work the barrels. A horse's attitude is hard to adjust once he becomes tired or bored.

8/

distribution should be balanced in the stirrups, directly under the rider, near the cinch. If you stand in the stirrups and sit straight down, the crotch area should be in the center of the saddle. This is your gravity point. If you'll think about "curling" your toes down in your boots before a run, this will help keep your feet and body in proper position for any movement.

Body positioning is very important in helping a horse through his fast turns. I stay up and over the horse as I approach a turn, riding ahead of the horse's motion. When I sit down in the saddle, this tells the horse to rate for the turn. He moves his hindquarters up under himself and positions his body. The horse's in-

1/ Working at a collected lope. . . .

2/

3/

side leg acts like a rudder as his outside hind leg drives his body forward. The power from the driving leg will actually help force the rider up and out of the saddle to maintain the forward motion. It is important to remember, however, that getting out of the saddle too early will possibly cause the horse to not finish his turn, and bow off the barrel.

Elbows should be kept close to your sides during a turn, with the rein hand brought back toward the hip area, rather than dropped out to the side. Remember that the rein is in the same hand as the turn, and the horse's nose should be tipped in the direction of the turn with the rein acting as a lead. The outside leg has more pressure in the stirrup, allowing the inside leg to act as a guide for the horse to turn around. The novice rider can exaggerate this position by standing to the outside as she slowly works the pattern.

RATING

Once a horse really begins to understand the movement involved in forming a pocket and turning, I'll begin to work on rate. A smart horse will probably think at this point, "There's a barrel. I'm going to have to turn, so I'd better slow down." But even a smart horse needs reinforcement, practice in adjusting stride when he's asked to rate, in order to slow down to turn a barrel. To begin, I'll walk up to a barrel, say whoa and pause before walking around the barrel, trot to the next barrel, say whoa and rate again. When I say whoa, I reinforce it two ways: first I sit deep in the saddle, and then I use the reins to reinforce the whoa. When he feels me sit like that, he's thinking about getting into the ground, and I don't have to pull as much on his mouth. He learns that when he's working the barrels, whoa in this instance doesn't mean stop, it means rate—shorten stride and prepare to turn. If I want a horse to stop, I'll use the voice command and take hold of him a little harder with the reins.

To continue work on rating, I'll go from a walk to a stop, then turn. If we're at a trot, we'll drop down to a walk be-

Working on rate. Sit down in the saddle and say whoa. The cones in this instance illustrate two possible points for rating, depending upon the individual horse, and the speed at which he is traveling.

3rd Barrel ◯ X
Rate 7-10'

2nd Barrel
X⟷X
◯ Rate 7-10'

1st Barrel
X ◯
Normal Rate
40'
Initial Rate → X
for "Chargey" Horse

The angle of the hips changes from this . . .

. . . to this, when asking for rate, or for a stop.

Completing a turn (photos above): look for the next barrel, scissor your legs (outside leg moves slightly forward; inside leg moves slightly back), while the upper part of the body twists toward the next barrel. At speed, the rider will have to be ready to resume a forward seat.

fore turning. If we're at a lope, we'll drop down to a trot. Later, during a run, we'll simply shorten stride, then turn. The momentum of the run will carry a horse through his turn; and eventually it's the run and proper positioning that will "sling-shot" him around a barrel.

I've seen girls lope up to a barrel, then speed up the horse for the turn. They think this movement makes a real quick turn, but all it does is make most horses high and silly as they approach a barrel. I feel the pressure in the turns should be backed off, allowing the horse to gather himself to push off automatically, making a quick turn.

It's important to realize that the faster a horse is traveling, the farther away from a barrel he'll be when you need to ask him for rate. When we get into the section on problems, you'll see that one of the main problems a barrel horse develops is "slicing" a barrel. And the way he learns to slice is by being asked to rate *too* far back. As the rider slows him down to make a turn, the horse drops in with his shoulder, and dives into the barrel. The diagram shows where I ask a horse to rate during slow work, and at speed.

While working on rate, I have confidence that the horse knows how to stop from the work we did with the stops and roll-backs. I know when I pick up the reins the horse is going to start looking for some ground to get into. I've been building on rate all the way through. How well he has learned his lessons will show up when he is ready to gallop through the barrels. At that time, if I pick him up to turn, and he's got too much speed, I'll work on exercises to reinforce that rate. I can easily go back to the foundation to work on rough spots.

GETTING FASTER

When the horse is walking, jogging, and loping nicely through the barrel patterns, I'll begin to look for a bit that will afford me the control I need for speed, and begin to sneak in a fast run every now and then. I'll use the no stop/no start routine, and jog through once or twice, just enough to where the horse feels warmed up and limber, but not enough to make him bored. I'll take him through at a lope, and if he feels nice and light, and seems to be paying attention, I'll gallop him through the course. Then I'll bring him back down the fence after I turn the third barrel, and drop down to an easy lope for one more trip through the barrels. I've sneaked in a fast run, and reinforced it with a slow run, before putting him away. The horse went fast and didn't even know it; he's not high. I've applied some pressure. The next time we work the pattern, he is less likely to become tense.

At speed, instead of having the horse carry a strong arc going into the first barrel, I'll run him straight to the point I want to rate before turning. The same applies for the other barrels. This makes it easier for the horse to turn at speed, rather than bending around the barrels as we did earlier in the training at the walk and trot. We're still going to ask for an arc but it is in the turn, not in the approach, and it's not going to be the extreme exaggeration we assumed before.

This doesn't mean, however, that after we've run in this pattern we don't go back and reinforce that nice pocket while working slowly. At slow work I'll almost always go straight to the barrel, then ask the horse to bend and arc around it.

SEASONING

After a horse gets to the point where he's solid on barrels at all speeds at home, I'll begin to work him only a couple of times a week. I'll haul to a neighbor's house, or maybe take him to

Advanced Practice Barrel Pattern

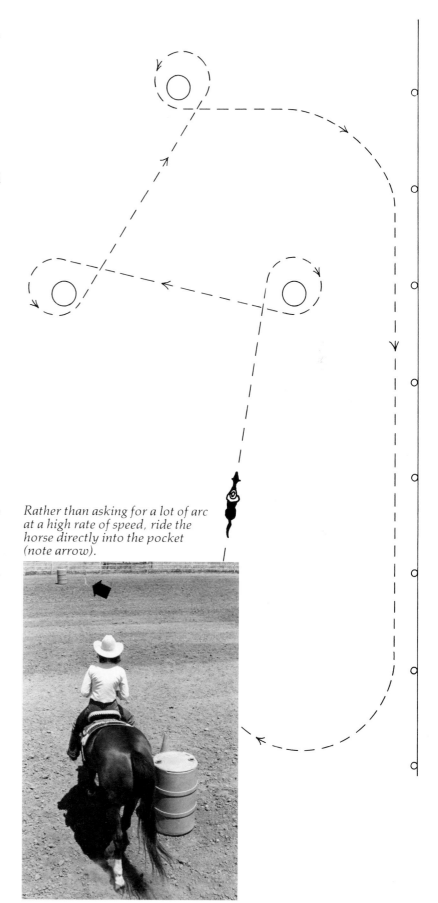

Rather than asking for a lot of arc at a high rate of speed, ride the horse directly into the pocket (note arrow).

The training foundation is important to a horse. It took four years to train Seven, but when I started hauling him he began winning right away.

a rodeo with an older horse I'm competing on. After the rodeo I'll set up the barrels and go through the pattern a couple times, to let him see that barrels grow in other arenas, not just his. A lot of times, a young horse will feel so solid in his own arena, but you take him somewhere else and it's new to him. That's the first step in seasoning the horse.

The rider needs to understand that this is a volatile time for a barrel horse. When you take him away he's under the stress from hauling, and all the noises associated with the road and rodeo, so give him a little extra consideration. Don't pressure him too much on a new pattern. And if he doesn't respond the way you think he should, be patient, finish the session and put him away.

I've found that it really does help a young horse to haul him with a seasoned old veteran. A horse like Stick (Leo's horse) has seen and done it all. He's calm, and he has a calming effect on a young horse who needs security.

The period of time it takes to make a barrel horse is going to vary, but I would say—from start to finish—about a year, depending on his attitude and how well broke the horse was initially. And then maybe six months to a year of seasoning follows that. If it takes any longer than that, the rider may want to think about replacing the horse or modifying the training program.

One thing about my horse Seven—it took me four years between rodeo schedules to train him, but once I started hauling him, he didn't need as much seasoning. He started winning right away. So, are you going to put in the time in your own arena and shorten the seasoning period, or cheat on time spent at home and spend more time on the road? I believe in training at home, and competing when I leave. For one thing, it's a lot more economical.

At my clinics, I teach my students to study my style of riding and training, and try it. Certainly there are parts of my style that will work for a lot of others. I also point out that I modify my style on each horse I ride. There are some horses that don't need as much pocket as others, so I close in the pocket. Other horses don't need as much bend, others need more rate.

Some moves are cut and dried: the horse has to run up to a barrel, he has to rate, he has to give you some pocket with his nose to the inside. But if he wants to go a little farther before he rates, or rate a little earlier, or whatever, that's fine. After I show him the basics, it's like I say, "Okay, you show me what you need to make a good horse." If I can live with it, I'll modify my style to fit the horse.

Anything good takes time, and foundation is so important to a horse. The mistake many girls make: they get a good run in the practice arena, so they enter the next rodeo. The horse may or may not be ready for the pressure—once his mind is blown, he'll be hard to bring back. It remains the rider's responsibility to know when her horse is ready for the pressure of competition.

When you're ready to leave the practice arena for a little on-the-road seasoning, it helps to haul a solid veteran along with the newcomer.

Riding inside the arena before the rodeo gives the horse a chance to get the feel of the ground. I don't want any surprises during my run.

7 CARE & CONDITIONING

EXERCISE

I like to build up to a four-mile workout, several times a week.

An application of fly spray during the summer months will help keep a horse comfortable, and his mind on the training or exercise session at hand.

The conditioning program is just as important as the training program. Training schools a horse for competition, while conditioning prepares the horse physically to withstand the rigors of the contest. Not only does a well-conditioned horse have a better chance of winning, he has a better chance of staying sound.

Once a horse is trained and seasoned, his work program should be switched so that conditioning is the primary focus of physical activity. When I'm getting a horse in shape, I'll start out slowly, and build up to a four-mile workout several times a week. The program means I'll walk the horse for one mile to warm him up, then go into an extended trot for one mile (usually posting in the saddle). Then I'll go into a controlled hand-gallop for another mile, and this is followed by a cooling down period: I'll walk for another mile or so until the horse is breathing normally, and the sweat is dried off. On a horse that is completely out of shape, I start with a half mile of trotting and a half mile of galloping. On off days, I'll do a little work in the arena. And he'll get one day completely off each week—usually the Monday following a

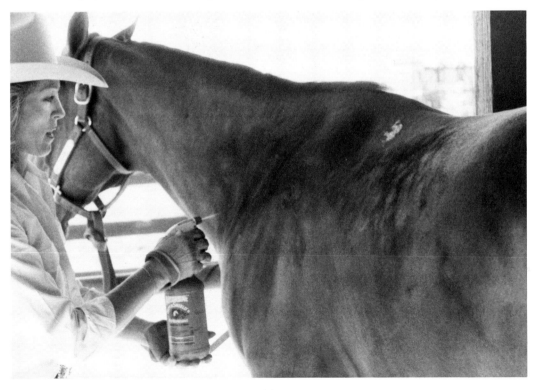

Hay net and buckets for traveling at top, along with an assortment of daily grooming supplies and tools.

rodeo weekend.

About every seven to ten days, if I'm not making several competitive runs during the week, I'll walk a mile, trot one-half mile, pick up a lope for one-fourth to one-half mile, and then sprint him—ask him for everything he has—for about 250 yards. Then I'll bring him down to a gallop, and ease down to a walk and cool him out. On these days he is getting exercised harder, but going less distance. What this does is increase his lung capacity, suck up his belly, and work on those muscles that a horse has to use to push and pull when he has to run hard in a barrel race.

It seems to take the muscles about 20 minutes of walking to come back off a strenuous exercise, even though the horse may look cool and is breathing normally. After that, he can be put away. If a horse doesn't get cooled off, he'll develop muscle soreness.

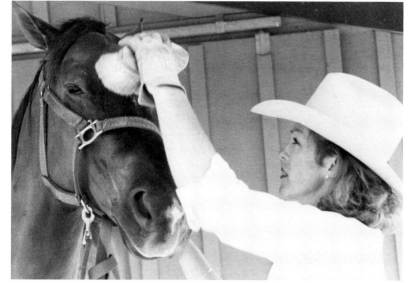

Use a soft brush for grooming around face and eyes.

65

A rubber scrubber is a handy tool to bring dirt and loose hair to the surface.

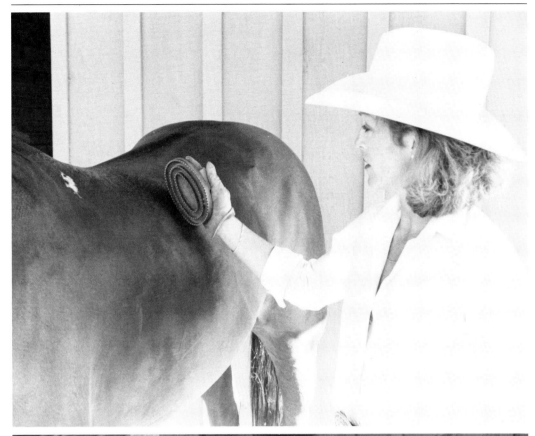

A rubber mit is good for cleaning around eyes and legs. It allows the groom to remove dead hair in places a rubber scrubber can't reach.

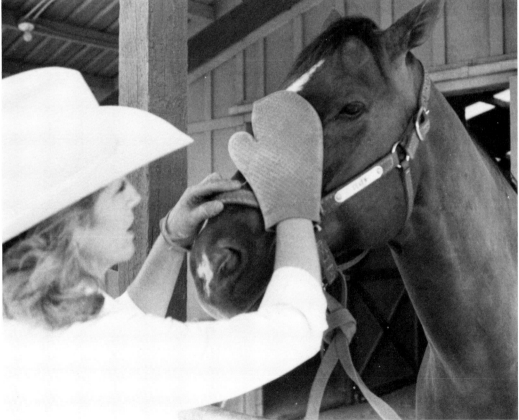

Use the soft brush and old fashioned elbow grease to brush away debris loosened by the scrubber.

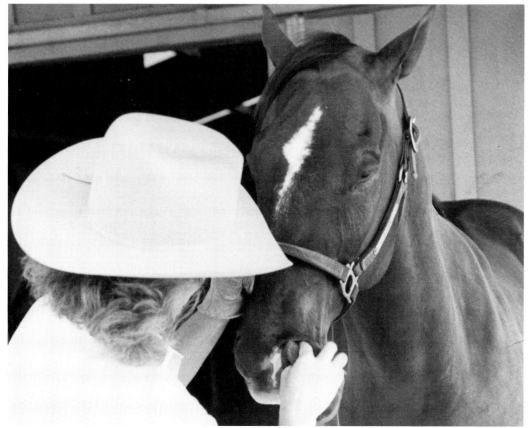

Use a sponge to remove dirt around eyes and nostrils.

Conditioners are great for helping to remove tangles from manes and tails.

A soft cloth sprayed with alcohol completes the grooming session. It removes excess dust, and brings out the sheen in the horse's coat.

One thing I want to stress is that any conditioning program can be as hard on an out-of-shape horse as the training program can be. And the horse that is just flat out of shape will possibly take 90 to 120 days to get back into good physical condition. So it's not a program to be rushed into. A horse that's in fairly good shape to start with will probably take an additional 30 to 45 days to get into top shape. It's not an overnight process.

If there is no gauge for distance available, I estimate it takes about 45 minutes to one hour for a good workout. Of that time, I'll build him up to a ten-minute lope. Remember, each horse is an individual and must be conditioned accordingly. Studies have been done on conditioning race horses and endurance horses, but when it comes to barrel racing, just how one goes about conditioning a horse to give everything he has for an 18-second run is up to the individual. We don't need our horses as fresh as race horses, nor do we need them in the same condition as an endurance horse. Age also is a factor. An older horse is harder to condition. It takes more time to keep him in top shape. A younger horse needs time off for his mind, and may take too much time to "ride down" if he is in excellent shape too early in his training.

This conditioning program obviously will be modified once a horse goes on the road to a lot of rodeos. You can't haul him for 10 or 12 hours, then unload and

Riding through the grapes. The dirt road that surrounds and intersects the vineyard across from our place is a great place to exercise.

ride four miles, and then compete. So I like to have my horse in good shape, and built up to this four-mile routine before the season gets underway. The program during the season will be maintenance— a lot of walking, some trotting, and a little galloping. If I've got a concentrated number of rodeos, I'll just walk the horse and keep him limber between runs.

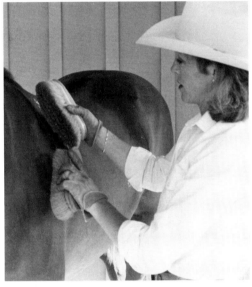

After a workout, I'll brush away any sweat marks.

A cool bath after a workout has got to feel good to a horse.

Sometimes a seasoned horse will gradually get "scotchy"—especially by fall. He'll be in top condition in the spring, then you leave and hit all the summer rodeos. When you bring him home after Labor Day, he's a little sour, burnt out on barrel racing, and not giving all he can, especially when he leaves the third barrel. That's when I'll take him back to the track and sprint him. Sprinting seems to free up a horse; he doesn't have to run and stop, run and stop. He gets to travel somewhere, and that often freshens him up and adds new interest to the barrels.

Even though a horse is making a lot of runs, he may gradually lose his wind without the long-distance workouts. When that happens, I'll sometimes take him to a training facility with an equine swimming pool, and let him swim for a week. This gives him a break from the routine and it's good for his lungs. Afterwards, we'll do some road work to recondition his legs since swimming does little to tone tendons.

At home feed is easy to keep consist-

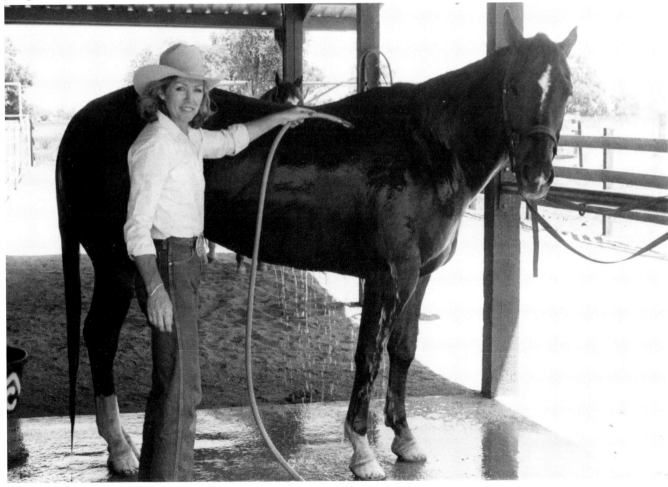

70

Top to right—rim shoe, cutting horse plate, racing plate. Other two shoes—barrel racing plate and polo shoe.

ent. We buy it from the same place, and have access to plenty of good alfalfa hay. When we're on the road, however, that's not always the case. Hay varies, but I try to stay consistent in the grain I feed. I'll feed a good-quality sweet feed that consists of corn, barley, and oats with a little bit of molasses; I cut this mixture half-and-half with whole oats.

My main supplement has vitamins and coat conditioners in it, and I don't think you can beat plain old corn oil or soy oil for the coat conditioner. I give up to a quarter of a cup in the grain once every other day. Usually, a couple of tablespoons is enough to really make his hair stay shiny and healthy looking. The oil not only conditions the coat, but has a laxative effect, replacing the need for bran, which is sometimes necessary, especially on the road.

When I've got him on the road, and he's going a lot of miles and making a lot of runs, or if the horse warms up flat and just doesn't seem to have a lot of life, and I'm sure he isn't sick (no tempera-

ture, no runny nose), I'll increase his grain ration.

If the horse begins to get too high or if I know I won't be riding him hard, I'll be sure to cut back on grain. You can't feed a horse a lot of "hot" feed unless he's working hard. If he isn't working, he may tie-up or even founder. It's wise to remember to feed a horse according to his needs. Obviously, a horse that travels will undergo more stress than a horse that stays home.

When I'm on the road, I also keep a horse on Lite Salt (low in potassium). At home, the horse has a salt block in the pen for free choice salt, but on the road I add one-half to one ounce of salt to his grain to keep him drinking water, and to help replace some of the salt his body sweats away.

SHOEING

I have my shoer put regular "cowboy shoes" or "rim shoes" on any young horse I start. If a problem later shows up

Feet should be cleaned before and after a ride, to dislodge any debris that has accumulated.

I like to apply hoof dressing to help keep feet moist and therefore prevent cracks. Like anything, this can be overdone; don't use hoof dressing so profusely and so frequently that the hoofs become too soft.

and the horse needs slightly different shoes, we'll take it from there. Horses will also often go through stages where they need different shoes during different stages of their careers.

When I first hauled Seven, he had a tendency to clip himself high inside his hind legs during turns. The inside hind leg would hit the other hind leg during a powerful, high-speed run. So my shoer put a trailer with a cork on the outside of his back shoes. That gave him more support in his turns and cured the slippage. About a year-and-a-half later, after running on a lot of hard ground, I discovered those corks were making him sore in his hocks and back. They were fine in soft ground, but caused too much drag on hard ground. So I took them off, and the shoer put on steel polo plates. They worked well for a while, but Seven is such a big, powerful horse that they did not offer him enough wall support. I switched back to a regular rim shoe. The polo plate is similar to a rim shoe; however, the inside rim is higher than the outside rim. This differs from the barrel racing plate, which has a higher outside rim. I like the polo plate because there seems to be less chance of the horse hurting himself if he happens to over-reach.

The whole idea of a rim shoe is to increase traction. Ironically, the best traction is "dirt against dirt," so the shoe has its best traction when the rims are filled with dirt.

I also like to have the shoer cup out the feet. This increases traction. I don't like to over-do the cupping, however. For example, race horses really have their feet cupped out a lot, but they're always running on nice ground. Rodeo horses might have to be warmed up on gravel or pavement; a deeply cupped hoof is more susceptible to stone bruises. I also think it's a good idea to square off the back toes, to help prevent over-reaching.

I do like to keep a horse set up in front a little straighter, and my shoer knows this. This helps a horse break over quicker in his stride. Consequently, he can leave a barrel more quickly. If you get those feet set too straight, it can also shorten the stride—it's a very fine line. I just want those toes filed back "a hair," rather than left out long. The slope of the hoof should still conform to the slope

72

of the pastern.

I also want the shoes "set full." A lot of shoers will put a slightly smaller shoe on a hoof, to avoid any "overhang." This gradually makes the foot smaller and can lead to contracted heels, and that's just one more problem.

If I'm on the road and have to have new shoes put on by someone other than my farrier at home, I'll have an extra set of shoes with me that have already been shaped especially for each foot on my horse. These can be easily nailed on by another shoer.

Remember not to correct the hoof too much. He should be shod as he stands—especially if he is an older horse. Different shoes work for different horses. One thing about rodeo—we can't put a certain type of shoe on a horse that is geared for only one type of running surface. We might run on grass, deep sand, heavy ground, hard ground. So I've learned to stay away from corks and exotic shoes.

I should add that I'm not a shoer, so I want a horseshoer in whom I have a lot of confidence. I like to develop a good working relationship with my shoer as well as my veterinarian. We're like a team. I have confidence in them.

WORMING & VACCINATIONS

I like to worm a horse four times a year—every three months. In the past I've alternated between paste and tube worming, but with the new improved pastes on the market, I now use paste entirely, and check up on the thoroughness of the worming with fecal samples analyzed by my veterinarian.

In the spring, I give the three-way shot: tetanus/sleeping sickness/flu. I'll follow up in six months with another flu shot. I give the flu shot to any horse I'm going to be hauling a lot. I think it's especially important to give the flu shot to a young horse because he hasn't built up all the resistance that an older horse has.

One more item not to be over-looked is to have the horse's teeth checked at least once a year. If his condition drops off, if he isn't eating like he should, if he starts fighting a bit he used to work in, he could need some dental work.

8 SOLVING PROBLEMS

When a solid horse quits working altogether, there's usually a reason. He's probably hurting somewhere.

If my horse makes a run and has a problem with a particular part of the barrel racing pattern, or doesn't work as well as I know he can, I'll give him the benefit of the doubt. Maybe he had an off day. If the problem continues, however, then I will work on it. When a solid horse quits working altogether, there's usually a reason—he's possibly hurting somewhere.

1/ It is useful to know how to apply a "Furacin wrap." This treatment is used to reduce swelling in lower legs—swelling caused by stress or an abrasion. First, clean the wound, then apply a thin layer of Furacin topical ointment. The Furacin, properly wrapped, will cause sweating, thereby reducing the swelling. Leave the wrap on for 12 to 24 hours; if another treatment is required after that, rinse the leg and repeat the procedure. If it is a fresh injury, cold bandaging may help reduce the amount of swelling before the wrap is applied.

I'll check for heat and/or swelling. I'll carefully go over his legs and feet. I'll check his back for soreness. If I can't find a problem, but I'm still not certain he is completely sound, we go to the veterinarian for his evaluation before I do much serious tuning.

Ground conditions are important considerations, too. If we make a run on slick ground and the horse slips and catches himself, he possibly could be sore somewhere for a day or two. We'll discuss more on ground conditions in the following chapter.

Anyway, if my horse develops a problem, and I'm sure there's nothing bothering him physically, I'll go to work correcting it before it becomes a real problem. Ideally, we'll go home to our own arena. But if we're far away, in the middle of a string of rodeos, then I'll just have to wait until we can find a time and place to work where we're not distracted. There's nothing worse than taking a horse back to the arena after a rodeo, to work on a problem, while five or ten other barrel racers are trying to work, too. Rather than add to the crowd, I'll put my horse away, and try to go out early the next morning when a lot of others aren't around. We can have a nice, quiet tuning session that way.

This is something I learned from Leo. I went through a stage many years ago when I'd be mad after a bad run, and Leo

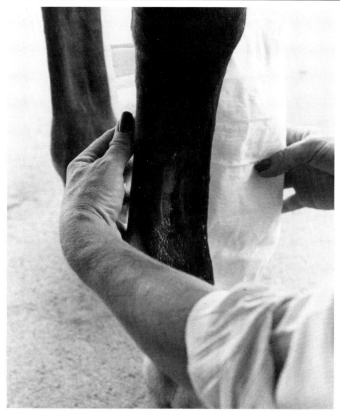

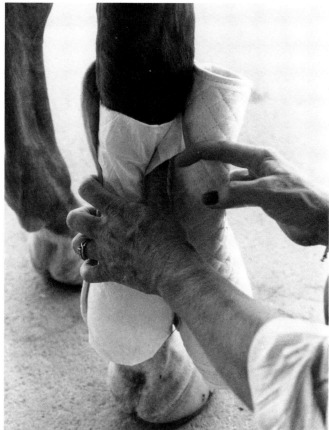

2/ Wrap the leg with a disposable baby diaper. Put the absorbant side next to the leg, so the moisture has somewhere to go as the medicine draws.

3/ Next, place a quilted pad around the diaper.

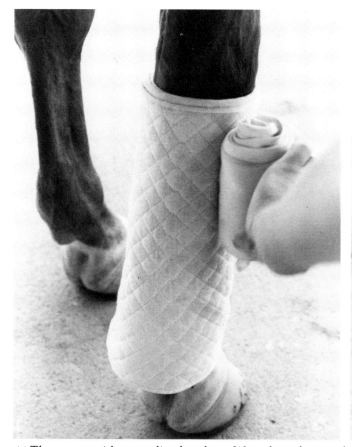

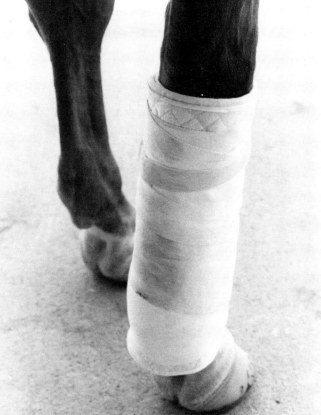

4/ Then wrap with a standing bandage. Wrap from front to back, clockwise on the right side of the horse, counterclockwise on the left, rolling the tendons to the inside. Start at the top and work down, then work back to the top and tie it off.

would say, "Hey, it's over. That run is done. Put your horse up for now, and then start building for your next run." That's good advice. Don't be mad after a bad run, analyze it, and try to figure out what went wrong and why.

I hate to see a barrel racer get so mad after a bad run that she can't even think straight. "What did you do?" someone will ask. Her head shakes; she's upset: "I don't know."

Possibly the horse didn't rate, so he ran by his barrels, or the rider rated him too early and caused him to slice. Whatever the problem, it needs work. On the other hand, what if he ran exceptionally well? Analyze that: Did you ride him "loose?" Did you push him hard to the first barrel? Think back on the run and learn from it—it'll make the next run better, and the competition more consistent.

CHANGING BRIDLES

Obviously, no changes should be made in head gear if your horse is working to your satisfaction. Changes should be made to anticipate or correct problems. If a horse is running through the bit or fighting it, first make sure it is properly adjusted, and not pinching or causing some other discomfort. Make sure it isn't a dental problem. If a change in bits is necessary, analyze the problem and select a bit that offers what you need.

If it's more bend and nose control you want, you might try a gag-type bit. But be aware that a gag bit may offer too much bend, forcing the horse onto his front end, sacrificing rate, and causing his hindquarters to sling out wide in a turn. If a horse has too much bend, try to stiffen him with a solid-sided bit, or

A tuning session for Seven. He's working in a gag bit.

perhaps even a hackamore bit.

A bridle with more control, like the polo bit, may help a horse that needs more rate; or a short-shanked bit or snaffle bit may be tried to free up a horse that is "scotchy" or has quit running into the bridle.

PICKING YOUR POINT

When you start a run, you want to travel to a point somewhere off the first barrel, where you'll ask the horse to rate, and set him up for his turn. Picking this point can be a problem, especially for beginners. Here's what happens: The rider knows where she wants to turn, and so she looks at that spot on the ground. Instead of traveling to that spot, however, they both anticipate the turn, cheating their pocket. They end up slicing the barrel.

To avoid that situation, pick your point before the run begins, and then look straight beyond that point to the fence or some other visible marker. Keep your eye on the far point during the approach. Although the horse is anticipating the turn, your upright body position will help him stay honest to the point where you begin the turn.

The same technique applies to the other barrels. A lot of horses will be scotchy going into the second or third barrel. That's probably because the rider looked directly at the barrel, and where you look is where you ride. So if I want my horse to run to the right of the second barrel, I'll look at that point, and then beyond that point to some visual reference on the fence. We should see each barrel with peripheral vision, but not look directly at them. Pick your points along the fences, and ride to those points.

A lot of pro barrel racers will walk a course on foot before the rodeo if they can't get in to ride first. They'll see where the first barrel is marked, and see the alleyway, so they've got two fixed points. Then they'll pick the point on the ground and look beyond the point to something more visual—the top of a stairwell, a sign, a letter in one of the rodeo banners hanging on the fence. This is where they will look during the run as they leave the alley and approach the first barrel.

The cones represent the line of travel to the first barrel. The middle cone, adjacent to the barrel, is the point I would actually rate and turn. But I won't be looking there. Instead, I'll look beyond to another point (third cone at top), and ride as if I'm going to turn there. This practice helps the horse honestly get to the proper turning point without anticipating.

77

1/ Tuning for a horse that wants to shoulder a barrel.

2/ Working at the trot, I'll ride up to the barrel, elevating my inside rein, and we'll turn in the opposite direction.

3/ We'll make a complete circle, come back to the barrel, then turn it correctly.

SLICING A BARREL

This is a two-fold problem. First, the horse is usually rated too early by the rider; once he rates, he is ready to turn, but he is still too far from the barrel. The rider kicks him back up for another stride or two. The horse has lost his momentum, closed in his pocket, and simply hits the barrel with his shoulder. Or, if he does miss the barrel, he'll still wind up out of position. He'll either run wide off that barrel, because his approach was too close, or there will be a dead spot where he has to collect himself on the back side of the barrel. This is called "veeing" a barrel.

Another rider mistake can occur during a training session in which direct reining is used. The horse is asked to rate too soon (first mistake); the rider then realizes the horse is going to slice the barrel, and consequently uses the outside rein to pull his nose and body away from the barrel (second mistake). This causes the horse to drop his shoulder even farther toward the barrel, and results in a slice. In this case, the rider should have used the inside rein to elevate the inside shoulder, bring the nose in, and emphasize the arc necessary to bend around a barrel.

4/ This helps to teach the horse not to anticipate. The idea is for him to run up to a barrel and wait for the rider to cue him for the turn. It is an exercise that can be utilized at a trot, lope or gallop.

78

NO RATE

It's usually the first barrel that most horses won't rate on their own. With a high-strung horse, one who's difficult to control, I'll usually be very consistent in getting him around the first barrel, until he becomes solid. I'll ride him two-handed if I have to in order to help him all the way around the turn.

If the horse is blowing by the first barrel in competition, I'll bring him home, check the bridle and make sure it is adjusted properly; check the tie-down and see if that's adjusted correctly. If it is, I'll either tighten it or switch to a more severe tie-down. It may be time to go to a chain tie-down. If the horse wants to run through the bridle, the chain will be there to back him off. A horse must respect his head gear in order for the rider to maintain control.

After I've checked the equipment, we'll go to the arena and work on rate. I'll lope the horse to the first barrel, sit down in the saddle and say whoa, then stop him dead in his tracks. If he gets in the ground good, I'll walk around the barrel and lope or trot him to the next barrel. If he doesn't want to stop, and kind of bounces with no stop on his mind, I'll hold him until he stops, roll him back to the left, providing it is a right turn, and trot or lope back down past the starting line, stopping into the fence.

Next, I roll him back to the right. This sets him up in the correct lead for a right-handed barrel course (and therefore, this procedure would be conducted in opposite directions for a left-hand course). I'll lope back to the barrel again and ask for a stop. If he doesn't get into the ground the way I want him to, I'll repeat the

Some horses may need to be rated farther up into their turns.

This cone, on the second barrel, demonstrates the rate point on the back side of the barrel. A horse is guided into his turn before he is asked to rate. This will position his hocks underneath him for a quick turn.

79

1/ Using the roll-back routine to work on rate. Note barrel at right.

2/ Horse is backed a few steps to put him on his hocks before the roll-back.

procedure; I might have to do this three or four times, so when I ride up there and say whoa, he's looking for a hole to get into.

Backing is another way to work on rate. Lope to the barrel, sit down on the horse, and stop him in an arc, adjusting the inside rein slightly shorter than the outside rein. If he bounces to a stop, I'll back him a few feet, pausing before I proceed around the barrel.

The severity of the problem will determine which exercise the rider should choose. The roll-back is good for problems on the first barrel with a more advanced horse. A green horse will normally respond to the backing.

3/ Roll back away from the barrel using direct rein and outside leg.

4/ *Trot or lope back to the arena fence . . .*

5/ *. . . before asking for another stop.*

6/ *Roll back in direction of approaching turn . . .*

7/ *. . . forcing horse to pick up the correct lead.*

81

8/ Again, we approach the barrel.

9/ Sit, say whoa, and ask for another stop.

10/ If he still doesn't have rate on his mind, repeat the exercise until he does.

PIVOTING ON THE FRONT

In this instance, the horse plants his front feet during a turn and pivots on them, slinging his hindquarters around the barrel. To correct this, I'll lope to the barrel, making sure my reins are gathered up properly. I'll carry a shorter direct rein, so I can keep his head set and bend his nose toward the barrel to help maintain the arc as we turn. I'll reinforce this with direct pressure with my outside leg. I can also bump him with my outside boot or spur behind the back cinch to help get his hindquarters underneath him. We'll continue to circle the same barrel at a lope, and if he still wants to pivot and sling his hindquarters, I'll slap him on the butt with an over-and-under or long training reins. Once I feel both his front and rear moving properly in a forward arc around the barrel, I'll go on to the next barrel. That's the reward. I don't want to continue to circle the same barrel once he begins to move correctly.

This positioning, making a horse drive up under himself, works for the left or right barrels. All you have to do is change hands and get ready for the problem you know you have. It's important to ride aggressively—be ready to correct the problem as soon as it occurs.

STIFFNESS

Occasionally, the older, seasoned horse will become "stiff." He won't bend around the barrel; he starts losing that nice arc he's been taught to carry in his turns. Be sure to put him in a bridle that gives you direct, lateral control, like a ring snaffle or Springsteen.

Go back to the exercises you used to teach him bend in the first place—the figure eight at a jog (pattern C), and the lope in a circle (pattern D) with the nose to the inside and then outside. The figure eight pattern usually makes a horse limber right away. If the horse still feels stiff, proceed to exercise B (loping) to exagerate the shoulder movements by straightening your elbow and raising your hand up along his neck. In other words, if you're loping to the left, raise your left hand—straighten your elbow and tip his nose upward. At the same time, you can bump him with the inside

For a horse that is strung out in his turns, circle a barrel at a lope, and spank his butt, if necessary, to get his hindquarters moving underneath him.

Continue to circle until the horse is moving around the barrel in a correct arc, driving forward with his hind end.

leg, and that will move his body over, reinforcing the arc.

It is important to make sure a horse's hindquarters are moving as freely as his front in all of these exercises. If the horse still resists these exercises, the rider can avoid a fight by taking him to the round corral and tying his head around (Chapter 5). This is usually a sure-fire attitude adjuster, and it allows the horse to correct some of his problems without resenting the rider.

THE SOUR HORSE

The sour horse, in this instance, doesn't want to enter the arena. He's probably been overworked on the barrel pattern, and feels he can avoid the confrontation if he refuses to go through the gate. This type of problem usually comes from inexperience on the part of the rider. The cure for this type of behavior is to ride the horse in and out of the arena periodically without running the barrel pattern. If he sulls up and wants to run backwards, get out the over-and-under and whack him across the butt until he moves forward. But when you do that—and this is especially important for youngsters to understand—don't pull on the reins at the same time. I've seen this happen a lot, and what it does is teach the horse to

If a horse tends to be scotchy, or over-anticipates his turns, I'll work him "by" his barrels at a trot and lope. I mentally pretend the first and third barrels are five feet farther down the arena and the second is five feet closer to the fence.

rear because he wants to get away from the pressure. That's why we offer them "a hole." The hole in this case is the arena. The reins are pushed forward, they're loose, and all you're doing is using them to guide the horse in the proper direction.

Once you get him in the arena, just let him stand. Talk to him, pet him, show him the arena isn't a bad place to be, get off, uncinch, and then walk him out. Something else to do with a horse that has a tendency to be sour is to work him in the opposite direction on the barrel course. When you switch him, it sometimes brings the horse back to listening once again for the rider's cues.

KEEPING THEM TUNED UP

Keeping horses working is often more difficult than training them in the first place. A rider must respect her horse and strive for his respect in return. This creates a bond that will carry both of you through the stressful situations that will be encountered in competition. I believe it's important to try to figure out a horse, and work with him to reinforce his idea of exactly what you expect from his performance. I believe in "training" at home, and "contesting" whenever the money is up. The pressure of competition will show whatever weak points need to be worked on between times.

It's important to keep the horse's movements feeling fluid. I believe more polishing can be achieved at a jog and lope than by asking for speed in the practice pen. If a horse tends to be scotchy or anticipates his turns too much, the rider can jog him past the barrel in an exaggerated turn. Remember to not overwork your barrel horse. Exercise him outside the arena as much as possible. A nice long trail ride is a good break for both horse and rider. Remember, too, that none of us will excel every time we compete. And a horse is no different. We are all entitled to have a few off days.

Once you have a "made" horse, I would very rarely show him the barrels at home. I'd just keep him happy and conditioned. I'd go to the barrels only to work out a problem. For a young horse, maybe work on barrels three or four times a week; and after every ten or twelve weeks of training, I'd give him a week or two off. It all helps to keep him fresh and willing.

WHIPS AND SPURS

I believe spurs and whips can create more problems for riders than they can solve. I caution inexperienced riders, especially, about overusing spurs. It's hard for most riders to use spurs effectively because they aren't always aware of where their feet are, or what the feet are doing. I ask the horse to move with the calves of my legs, but if I have to *help* him to move, I'll use my heels. This keeps his mind on pleasing me, instead of wringing his tail or fretting about when he's going to get gouged with a spur. If a rider isn't responsible with her feet, and continually hits her horse with spurs inadvertently, then she definitely shouldn't have spurs on her boots.

A final thought for this section: Not every horse and rider combination will hit it off, or get along well together. Call it a personality clash, but I've seen the situation where a horse works for one person and not for another. If an impossible situation becomes obvious, the smart rider should get out before she or the horse, or both, get hurt. The bottom line is enjoyment and profitability. If you can't get either of these it may be time for a change.

Standing tied inside the arena helps build a horse's patience.

A walk always helps keep a horse happy and relaxed.

85

9 HAULING AND WINNING

One way to help guard against accidents is to make sure the horse is traveling in a safe trailer with a stout hitch.

BE PREPARED

Travel preparations are much the same for me whether I'm getting ready to go to one rodeo or a string of rodeos. Whether I'm traveling alone or with another barrel racer, or with Leo, I always load feed and water buckets, hay and grain, a summer sheet and winter blanket (because even in summer, a winter blanket can be handy for a horse at some of the mountain rodeos that get those sudden, chilling thunderstorms).

I also put leg wraps on my horse every time I haul him. Leo never puts wraps on his rope horses, and they get along fine, but I feel better if they're on. I wrap for a little tendon support, and for protection; I think in an accident my horse would be more protected with the wraps on than he would with no wraps. If you choose

to use leg wraps, make sure you learn how to apply them correctly. An improperly wrapped leg can cause tendon bows. Therefore a beginner should not attempt a support wrap without an initial hands-on demonstration.

I also pack my own "vet kit"—a tackle box filled with a variety of first-aid materials and drugs I can use in case of injury—something to help my horse while I'm waiting for the veterinarian to arrive. Most of the places we go are big enough to have a good horse practitioner in the area, but the vet kit is really the best insurance for when something happens out in the middle of nowhere. That's just being prepared. The preparation of a layman's kit should be solely up to the veterinarian and his willingness to teach you how to use these drugs. The drugs he will give you in most cases may

The Camarillos' three-horse slant gooseneck trailer with tack compartment.

86

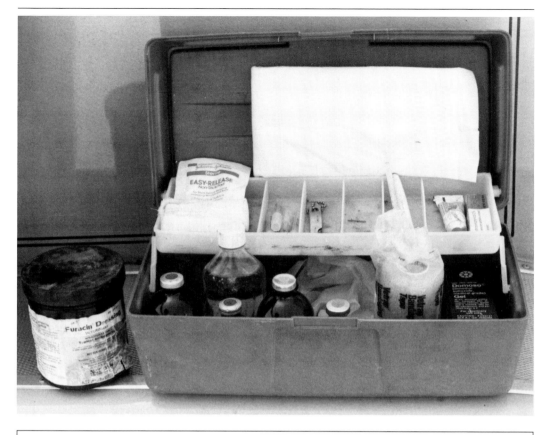

The 'vet kit' is the best insurance for when something happens out in the middle of nowhere, and a veterinarian can't be summoned immediately.

A professional horseman who spends a lot of time on the road should maintain a well-stocked first-aid kit, in case an emergency arises in which a veterinarian cannot be consulted or summoned immediately. Here's what I stock:

1/ Bandage material—Telfa pads for cuts, cotton or gauze rolls, Furacin, vet wrap and tape (to secure pads).

2/ Diaper or plastic wrap to administer a leg sweat.

3/ Small, sharp scissors.

4/ Betadine scrub to clean a wound before dressing.

5/ Banamine or Butazolidin, for relief of pain associated with colic or other disorders requiring this type of treatment.

6/ Acepromazine, to tranquilize a horse in the event of an accident in which the horse must be kept calm until a veterinarian can be summoned for treatment (a trailer accident, for example).

7/ 12-cc syringes.

8/ 20-guage, 1½-inch needles for intravenous or intramuscular injections. Note: these needle sizes would not be useful for administering thicker drugs, like antibiotics.

These drugs are restricted by law for use by, or on the order of, a licensed veterinarian. Most people won't be able to stock a kit with all these drugs, just as most horse people aren't qualified to give an intravenous injection. But this is an example of the type of kit most professional horse people have access to.

Again, it depends on a person's needs, willingness to learn, and willingness on the part of the horse practitioner to teach a professional horse person how to provide more than minimal care for his or her own horse in the event of a real emergency.

not be available over the counter.

One way to help guard against accidents and injuries is to make sure that the horse is traveling in a safe trailer with a stout hitch. If you have any doubts about the safety of your rig, consult a horse trailer and hitch specialist in your area. Many times this will be a local trailer sales and service person.

I always try to keep a trailer in good condition. If you have an older trailer, you want to make sure the floorboards aren't rotting, and that there are no sharp objects inside the trailer that can cause injury; I don't want any broken welds. I make sure the wheel bearings are packed regularly with grease by a knowledgeable mechanic.

I also like good padding on the floor. I've used foam and carpet pads under the rubber mats. Aside from the cushioning effect on legs, the extra padding helps insulate a trailer. That floor can get pretty hot traveling down the highway on a summer day. Another type of padding that's easier to replace is wood shavings. The shavings absorb heat and moisture, and I think a horse urinates more willingly with shavings because there is little splash on his legs. Sometimes, when it's real hot and dusty, I'll sprinkle down the shavings with water before I load up.

We have a gooseneck with a three-horse slant—three stalls in the trailer that are built for horses to stand at an angle to the road—and this is the trailer I

The trailer, bedded with wood shavings for a more comfortable ride.

Trailer hitches and balls should be stout and firmly attached (welded/bolted) to the frame of the towing vehicle. If in doubt about your hitch, consult a trailer maintenance garage in your area.

prefer. If I'm traveling alone, and not going cross-country to a lot of rodeos, I'll pull a two-horse trailer for fuel economy. But on longer trips, especially, the horses seem to ride easier and stay fresher riding at an angle. It's easier for them to keep their balance at an angle, rather than standing straight with the towing vehicle.

On long trips, I try to find a safe place to stop and unload about every four to five hours. I want to give my horse a chance to get out of the trailer and move around for a few minutes, and maybe have a drink of water. Rodeo horses are accustomed to hauling—loading and unloading—so there isn't any extra stress involved for them. I think a short break from the highway is good for all of us.

When I get to a rodeo, my first consideration is my horse. I want to unload him and, ideally, put him in a stall if we have plenty of time before the performance. If it's time to feed, I'll feed him, but I won't give him a full feeding if he's going to be running in a few hours. At least he'll be able to rest, to have a drink of water, and just relax from the trailer ride.

A lot of rodeos have evening performances, and if I've drawn up in one, I like to arrive at the rodeo grounds around 5 or 6 p.m. That gives me time to get a horse put up, park the trailer, check into

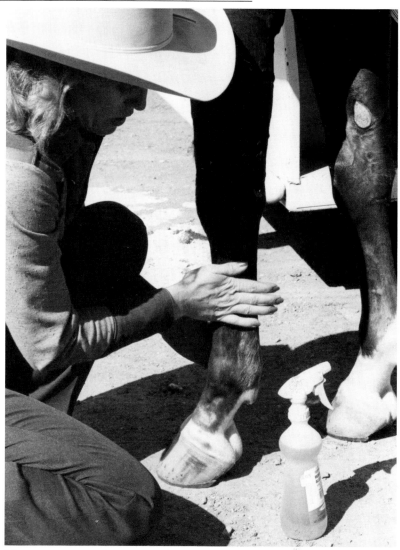

The importance of any superficial leg bracer is not necessarily its content, but the stimulation to the area created by hand rubbing. This extra care keeps the rider aware of the condition of her horse's legs.

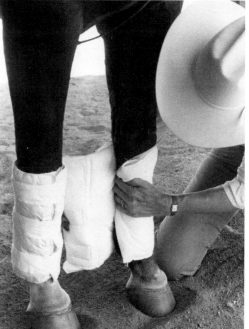

For short trips (one to two hours on the road), I'll put on velcro shipping boots. These add protection, but offer little leg support.

For longer trips, to support the legs and prevent "stocking up" while standing, I'll start with the alcohol bracer, then apply a quilted wrap held in place with a track bandage.

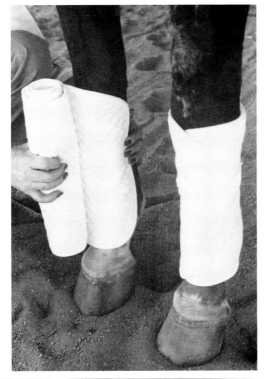

Remember to wrap the right leg clockwise, and left leg counterclockwise. This pulls the tendons to the inside.

The bandages are applied from the top of the leg to the bottom, working back up the leg until you come to the end of the bandage. Make sure any tension is applied by pulling bandages across the front of the leg. This will prevent excessive pressure from being applied on the tendon area.

a hotel, and get back to the arena about an hour before the rodeo starts. I've probably had a late lunch, maybe at 2 p.m., and I don't want a large meal before I compete, so I might have a cup of soup or a salad before going to the rodeo grounds. When I arrive, I'll go to the rodeo office and pay the entry fee, and pick up a day sheet (program insert) with the schedule of events. This will tell me exactly when we run barrels; I'll be ready when it's my turn, and I'll know the order in which we run. This is all part of being prepared.

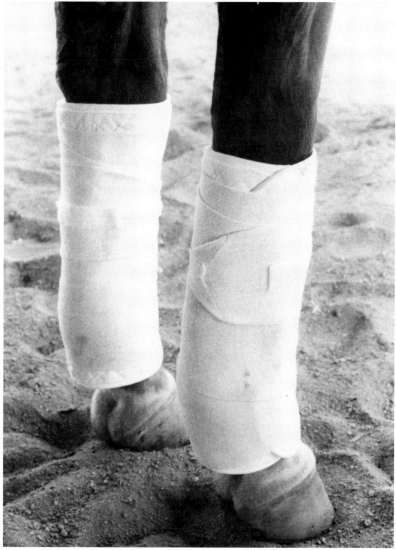

Bandages should be neatly applied with no wrinkles, and after all four legs are wrapped in this fashion, the horse is ready to load.

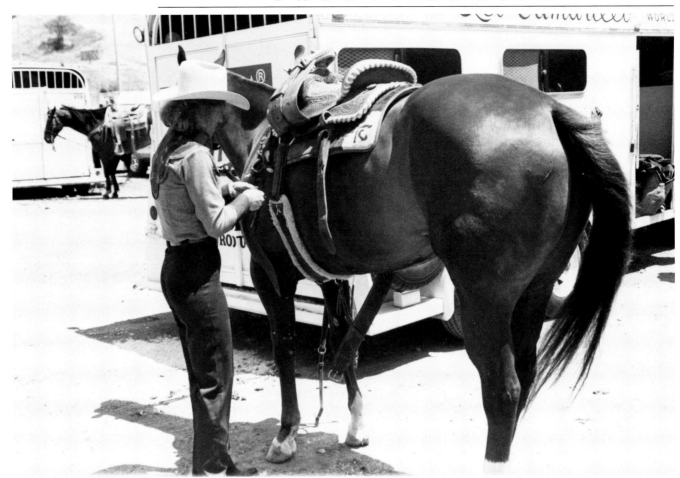

Grooming and saddling procedures at the rodeo are much the same as they are at home. Rubbing alcohol is used, in a spray bottle, after a run to help clean sweated areas.

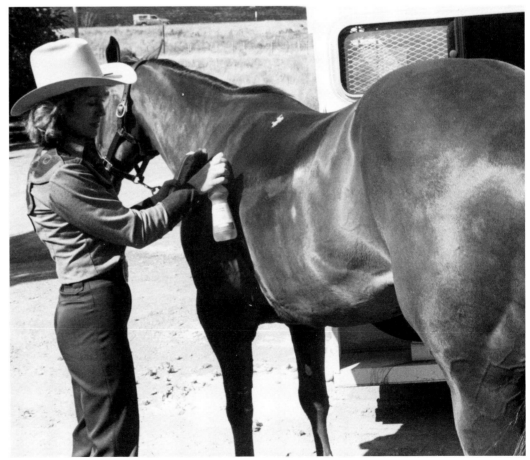

THE WARM-UP

The warm-up period can make or break your run. Actually, you can warm a horse "up" or ride him "down." A younger horse may need more loping than an older, seasoned horse. So, it's important to know the horse, to know when he's listening to you, to know when he peaks, and when he's ready to compete. Imagine his peak as the top rung on a ladder. You want to take him to the rung just below the top, and save the top rung for the actual run. It's up to the rider to be physically and mentally prepared if she and her horse are to make their best possible run.

I'll usually spend about 45 minutes warming up, but again this time can vary among horses. Of the 45 minutes, nearly 35 minutes will be spent just walking. On my horse Seven, I'll walk him until he urinates—that's a sign I recognize in him that tells me he is ready to complete the warm-up and then compete. Other horses will have other signs that show you they're ready to proceed with trotting, then loping.

From that point I will jog him about five minutes. If he's been kind of flat and hasn't really been running lately, I'll long-trot him, posting in the saddle to extend his stride. But if he's too high, I'll stay seated on him, and make him collect himself at a jog. Toward the end of

Here's the sign I look for in Seven. After he urinates, I know he's ready to finish the warm-up and compete.

It's always a good idea to get into the arena for a ride before the rodeo, if possible. Even just a few minutes inside will familiarize the horse with the surroundings, and give you a bit of that "home court" advantage when you make your run.

this period I'll incorporate a couple of my exercises. One will be a little figure eight with the nose in and then the nose out to limber his shoulders. After that I'll break him into a lope, and probably lope 100 yards in one lead and 100 in the other. There's a certain feel of limberness I'm looking for, and when it comes during this phase, it's obvious to me.

I plan to have the warm-up completed one event before the barrel race. I use that event for the horse to catch his breath while I check his feet, put on his protective boots, re-set my saddle, and get my own mind ready to compete. As the barrels are placed in the arena, I'll re-mount and slip rubber bands around my feet. I place a rubber band around each foot and stirrup, just for insurance. There's always a possibility, maybe in one run out of 20, where a rider can lose a stirrup during the course of a run. The rubber band prevents this from happening, and yet it will break easily in the event of an accident.

There's nothing worse than being late to compete, but if I find I've started the warm-up too soon—the rodeo is running slower than expected—I'll just stop and sit for a few minutes, then continue. I want the horse ready to run; I don't want to keep working him until he's reached his peak and begins to flatten out. Finding a good place to warm up

I like to wear spurs when I make a competitive run, but I'll first wrap the rowels with a little strip of vet wrap. This protects the horse from injury in case I unintentionally spur too hard.

Just before I make a run I'll place a rubber band around each foot and stirrup in this fashion—to help make sure I don't lose a stirrup. In the event of an accident, of course, the rubber bands would break free.

The over-and-under is laid across my leg just before I make a run.

Turning the second barrel during a competitive run. Remember to look for the next barrel as you complete the turn.

can be difficult, but you do the best you can. All too often the only place to warm up is a road or parking lot behind the arena.

If this is the case, I'll usually do as much walking as I can to keep my horse limber before a run. When it's my turn to run, I'll have my hat pulled down, and I'll be mentally ready to compete. I will have already picked my point to the first barrel (Chapter 8, "Picking Your Point"), and modified areas in my run to adapt to the existing arena conditions. My main thought, going to the first barrel, is to ride aggressively, and to make sure the horse rates for the turns. If a rider is going to have a problem with rating, it will probably be with the first barrel. After the first turn, I usually have to think only about competing for the rest of the run. There's a big difference between riding a horse through a pattern for training purposes, and riding him to win. In com-

petition, I want to rely on the horse to do his part, to show me what he's learned from the training sessions. I want to ride to the best of my ability, trying not to hinder the horse.

As I go into the first turn, I'll sit down in the saddle. On the back side of the turn, I will scissor my legs, as my upper body and head directly face the point I want to arrive at for my second barrel. The same body movements apply rounding the second barrel and the third. After I've crossed the finish line, I'll shift my weight back down in the saddle and ask for a stop. If there is enough length in the arena, it's best to ease the horse to a stop rather than jerk him to a sliding stop.

It's a fast life for sure, when you spend perhaps the better part of a day traveling to a rodeo and warming up for a competitive run that's over in something like 17 seconds.

Good conditions: inside the Astrodome during the Houston Livestock Show Rodeo in 1979.
Photo by Ken Springer

DON'T BEAT YOURSELF

When I pull into a rodeo, I'm not too concerned with checking the go-round times of any barrel racers who have gone before me. Barrel racing is so competitive that you've got to make a whale of a run regardless of what the other times are. What I'm concerned with is not beating myself. I want to make my best run, and I know that my best run is hard to beat.

There are a number of barrel racers, at any time, who are capable of making a great run. What I want to do is try to make that good consistent run I'm capable of making, and then let everybody else try to beat me.

I might check the times in an average, because if the ground is somehow less than ideal to run on, I want to know whether I have to go for broke on the next run, or maybe just make sure I don't hit a barrel. There are some ground and arena situations that are

conducive for hitting barrels. Deep, sandy ground, with barrels set close to fences, can cause this to happen; the Colorado Springs arena is one example. It takes a real aggressive rider to get through the course; you don't think about turning, you think about riding as hard as you can the entire run. The more momentum you can build, the better chance you have of getting through the course without knocking down a barrel. With the barrels close to the fences, the second you let up to give the horse a chance to rate and turn, he'll see the

closeness of the fence, and often turn too early, slicing or hitting a barrel.

The same situation occurs in the indoor rodeos. The horse feels a little more closed in, I think, and he has a tendency to perform a little snappier. Again it takes an aggressive rider to get through the smaller courses that are set up in the indoor rodeos. I'll be used to running a 17-second standard course in the outdoor arenas in California, and then I'll go to a smaller indoor arena like that at Baton Rouge, where I'll have to be 15 seconds to win anything. Your horse has

Bad conditions: at a WPRA-approved jackpot in San Angelo, Tex., in 1979. "The ground was hard, the weather cold, and a rain shower began as Sharon turned the second barrel," noted photographer Ken Springer.
Photo by Ken Springer

to be sharper, and you've got to be a lot snappier, because everything is happening faster. Here's the best part: When you return to the larger arenas, you'll be riding better than ever.

When we consider the ground alone, we need to determine whether it's hard, or deep, or sandy, or muddy. All of this will influence the competition, and that's

I can't control ground conditions at other arenas, but I always try to keep our home arena in good shape.

why it's important to enter the arena beforehand, if possible, and get a feel for the course. You determine what type of run to make by knowing your horse's limits. Some horses are great on bad ground (muddy, slick, or exceptionally cloddy). You can just let them go and they'll take care of themselves and the riders, too. Others aren't quite as arena-wise.

If you get inside the arena beforehand, and you have some doubts about the ground, lope your horse around. If he feels like he can't really handle it slow, he probably won't handle it going fast. But make up your own mind. Don't let another barrel racer psych you out with a lot of groaning about how terrible the ground is. In other words, don't beat yourself.

Occasionally, however, you'll have to sacrifice a run. Maybe one section of barrel racers already ran on good, fast ground the day before. Then a downpour of rain hit and turned the arena into a lake. In that case, you know the odds are against any winning times being made in the mud, so don't ask your

horse for that extra bit of effort. What I'll do is let my horse set the pace, and avoid the possibility of him slipping and injuring himself.

THE COMPETITION

I like to run against competition. I believe there's a time to learn, a time to gain confidence, and then the time comes to get out in the world and run against some good competitors. You'll ride only as good as your competition, and that's a habit hard to break. If you go to a barrel race where you only have to be 18 seconds flat to win, you'll probably be 18.5. But if you have to be 17.4, there's a chance you'll be 17 flat. It's easy to let down your guard a bit if the competition looks easy. If you go into a race and know it's going to be tough to win, you'll be ready to ride as aggressively as you can, because there's no other choice. Once a barrel racer starts entering tougher competitions, she'll find that she gets tougher, too, especially if she utilizes her runs, learns from them, and learns from watching other good barrel racers.

That brings up another point. When I go to a barrel race, if I'm not up during a particular performance or section of competition, I'll watch the runs if it's convenient, but I don't sit and pay attention to a whole barrel race. There will be very few girls whom I'll watch. And it's the same way if I'm up, ready to compete. I might be the sixth runner on the list, and I'll glance up at a good barrel racer and watch her. You could ask me, after the rodeo, "What did Martha Josey do?" Well, I could say she made a good run, but couldn't necessarily tell you her time. I watched her, but I didn't think about her run that much. What I did do, however, is instill a good picture in my mind. I watched a good run, then it was my turn to compete, and I had a positive mental attitude.

But if I would have watched several runs ahead of mine and seen one rider slice a barrel, one knock down a barrel and whip on her horse's ears, and another rider run off the course . . . well, I probably would have had a negative attitude, subconsciously. That's why there are very few runs at a rodeo that I'll really pay attention to. This practice is es-

pecially important for young riders; it helps prevent them from getting psyched out.

Don't be intimidated! A rookie, especially, can go to a barrel race with her horse—her partner from the backyard; she probably doesn't have a fancy trailer or a name-brand saddle, and might not be outfitted the way she would really like, but she's still pretty proud of what she's got. Her horse looks fit and well groomed, and she presents herself well. The two of them have worked hard to prepare for the competition. Then, after paying her entry fee at the rodeo office, her finger goes down the list of entries posted on the wall—*and there's half the top 15 there.* She suddenly thinks, "Gosh, I don't have a chance." Don't feel like that. At any time, any good horse can be outrun.

She should take advantage of the opportunity to watch those top competitors. Watch how they handle their horses: how they warm up, how they make a run, and what they do with a horse after a run. And then she should make her run and learn from it. If a girl can't make the same run at a rodeo she can make at home, she needs to ask why.

If you get nervous before a run, just remind yourself that you've entered for a reason—you felt ready to run when you entered, and nothing has changed. In that case, enjoy your run. Greg Ward of Tulare, Calif., the cowhorse and cutting horse trainer, told me something I've never forgotten: "You can go and worry about the competition," he said, "and worry about whether your horse will work, and whether you've got the right bridle, and wonder if the cinch is too tight. But if you've done your homework, you should be able to go out and just enjoy your run." I agree. It's not worth it if you don't enjoy it.

TRAVELING

When I'm rodeoing, I want things done my way, and I want them done efficiently. I don't have time for irresponsibility, and won't travel with anyone who feels differently. If I traveled across the country with someone who was going for different reasons, I'd probably arrive either so frustrated I couldn't think, or so insecure I couldn't beat anyone. So I'll travel with a strong competitor who thinks the way I do: "When I get there, I'm going to beat someone." If I have a travel partner like that, it makes the trip enjoyable and a lot easier to manage.

When you first start in this business, it's important to ask the other women things like how do you enter, where's the good ground, and so forth. Just walk up to some of them, especially in the summer when there are a lot of rodeos, and say, for example, "Listen, I'm thinking of going to the Colorado county fair circuit. What do you think about that?" Undoubtedly the reply will be, "They're tough, it usually rains, and the ground is bad." You might ask about other alternatives. You don't have to take anyone's advice, but at least you'll have some information to help make your own decisions.

There are some barrel races where you don't want to enter for the first runs if possible, and some where you don't want to be up at the end. It's all because of the ground conditions, and that's why it doesn't hurt to ask around. Most of the women will be more than happy to help you. Actually, I always feel complimented when someone asks for my opinion.

The ground can vary during the

course of a rodeo. Maybe the arena hasn't been used for a long time, and it's worked up once prior to the first performance. The ground isn't very good to run in initially, but by the last performance, it's been worked over several more times, and then it's nice. A lot of times you can't know that ahead of time; you take the luck of the draw.

Another example: At Albuquerque, we know they run the slack on a Thursday. They'll run 75 team ropers, 75 calf ropers, and 75 steer wrestlers, and by the time they are ready for slack in barrel racing, the ground will be hard. So it's tough to compete on that ground against girls who will be up that night. After the slack, the ground will be worked up again with a water truck and disk, and it'll be great to run on. Things like that you learn from experience, and you try to enter around them.

You won't have any say as to whether you're up first or last in a performance, but by entering through the PRCA's PROCOM entry system, a lot of times you can request and receive the performance in which you want to compete.

IN PERSPECTIVE

To win a world championship these days, a woman has to have either a special horse who's born to be a winner—that rare individual who will run on three legs if he has to; or she has to be a great cowgirl who can consistently get that extra effort out of a good horse. In either case, the champion invariably must also have a partner who wants her to win the title as much as she does. That someone can be a spouse or parent who is willing to go all out driving, helping to care for the horse, and taking care of a lot of responsibilities that go with rodeoing. If you wind up in a situation like that, great. If not, you can still be a win-

When you're winning, it seems so easy. But when a cold spell hits, it's a feeling like, "How did I ever win? It seems so hard. . . . " Patience and determination will help turn the cold spell around.

Sometimes, too, a person will try too hard. A horse isn't winning, so you go to the vet to see if he's sore, before you go to the arena for tuning and bridle changes. If that doesn't work, you analyze his feed . . . you're fishing for a reason. In reality, sometimes a rest for both horse and rider, away from the daily routine, does more good than anything else.

ner and receive a lot of personal satisfaction on whatever level of competition you choose, whether it's weekend gymkhanas, regional contests, or professional competition around the country. Do your training and homework, then go out there and enjoy your competition.

Competition Barrel Pattern

Pocket

Rate

Rate

Pocket

Pocket

Rate

Start / Finish

This diagram shows important points a rider must consider during her run. During competition, the horse and rider should run directly into their pockets. This makes it easier for a horse to turn at a high rate of speed, instead of the forward, sideways arc we ride when we are training and tuning.

Rate points show alternatives for the rider to sit down and cue her horse for the turn. The arrows closest to the barrel will be used by older, more seasoned horses that need to be pushed up into their turns.

The amount of pocket the rider will ask for is also an individual measurement that is important to maintain for the horse to start his turn and still leave close to the barrel.

This distance varies

Barrel

This distance doesn't vary

1/ Into a turn. . . .

2/ *I'm sitting deep in the saddle, and literally leading my horse's nose around the barrel. Note the slack in the outside rein. A finished horse will lose his dependency on the brace rein.*

3/ *Seven uses his inside hock as a rudder, while the outside hock acts as a driver. As my body scissors to look toward the third barrel, I make a snappy turn.*

4/ *As Seven coils to spring away from his turn, you can see how much a horse pushes with his hindquarters and pulls with his shoulders to get through a turn. At high speed, this is a difficult maneuver for any athlete.*

5/ Although I'm anxious to ride as aggressively as possible in order to shave every hundredth of a second off my time, I remember to stay seated in order to help my horse complete his turn. Getting up from the saddle too early can cause a horse to bow off the barrel.

6/ As Seven leaves the barrel, I jump my body a stride ahead of the horse, throwing myself forward in the saddle. This keeps me off his head and helps him to drive away from the barrel.

7/ *An aggressive rider should be able to hustle her horse in between barrels. I like to do this as I leave one barrel in order to build my momentum to carry me through my next turn. Hustling the horse early will give the rider more time to set up the horse for the next turn.*

8/ Staying up and over my horse, I push him home, urging him on with the over-and-under, if necessary. Usually, I just wave the over-and-under at the horse; however, when I do want to use it, I do so in rhythm with his stride. The whip should strike the horse when his front feet are off the ground. This will increase his stride.

9/ *Don't let up until you're sure you've crossed the finish line. I've seen races lost by riders who let up too soon.*

10 SURVEY OF WINNERS

Great horses are a gift. They come along maybe only once in a lifetime. In barrel racing, they have a common denominator: an abundance of speed, athletic ability, and most important, the desire to excell that can't be taught. Once a great individual has been discovered, it's the responsibility of the rider to be aware of what she has, and help him to develop accordingly. Here are some of the great horses and competitors I've admired and enjoyed running against. **Photos, unless indicated otherwise, are by barrel racing's Dean of Photographers, Ken Springer.**

Martha Josey on Sonny Bit-O-Both. Martha remains one of the greatest cowgirls and competitors I've ever seen in any horse-related event. Martha has competed on several great horses in her career, which explains why she was inducted into the Cowgirl Hall of Fame. Sonny was the first horse to win both the American Quarter Horse Association world championship in barrel racing, and the WPRA championship in the same year.

Carol Goostree on Dobre. He was a big horse with a long stride, and had the ability to gather for quick turns. He could really leave a barrel and run home with an extraordinary amount of speed. The combination of Carol, her husband Phil, and Dobre, made a very intimidating team. Carol took the 1979 world title.

Jerri Mann and Doz. This horse was competitive until his retirement at age 18, which qualifies him as one of the all-time top "horses with the most heart." His long and prosperous career, combined with Jerri's aggressive nature, ability, and natural timing, made them among the most consistent competitors I've ever run against.

Charmayne James and Scamper are real crowd-pleasers, and can give youngsters a strong desire to become barrel racers. The horse has that innate desire to excell, coupled with his strong athletic ability; and Charmayne lets him perform to the utmost of his ability. She, too, has an unusually strong determination to win. She isn't intimidated by the older, more experienced competitors, or by the pressures of professional competition. She's a tough hand who won her first world championship in 1984.

Jimmie Gibbs Munroe and Billy. What hasn't been written already about the great, late horse Billy? He had it all—talent, speed, and heart. In my book, he was one of the best all-around athletes barrel racing has seen to date. To top it off, Jimmie has the ability as a rider to create a desire in whichever horse she rides that makes them look as though they love what they're doing. Jimmie won the world title in 1975.

Lynn McKenzie and Magnolia Missile. Among his talents, this horse had a great first barrel—he could run to it and get around it faster than any horse I've seen. The fact that Missile was an outstanding futurity horse, and went on to win two world championships for Lynn (1978 and '81) is a tribute to his ability and desire. Lynn has "retired" him now to her daughter Wendy. "I always knew I had something special in Missile," Lynn said. "He was a gift to me and my family from God."

117

Jan Hansen admits that her form on her great horse Bandit wasn't the most stylish. But his natural ability and desire, combined with her talent to not interfere with his performance, made the combination in their day literally unbeatable. Jan was world champion in 1982.

Connie (Combs) Kirby and Joak—what a great team these two made! Joak has a naturally great first barrel and ran exceptionally hard off the third barrel. He was also a smart stud—tenacious, aggressive, kind of ornery—and it took a smart, highly-skilled horsewoman to ride him and keep him working. Connie was world champion in 1976.

Sharon on Charlie, Leo's ex-calf roping horse, at Spring Creek, Nev., 1975.

Riding Seven at the 1979 Sierra Circuit Finals.
Photo by Jim Fain

Seven was injured prior to the 1982 National Finals, so Sharon borrowed a horse from Jerri Mann for the competition. The mare is named Cowgirl.   **Photo by Jim Fain**

Basic theory and exercise have made my horse Seven a solid winner for a good many years. New competitors who are winning, however, often believe that they have found the key to training a barrel horse. But if they stay in the business long enough, they learn that replacement prospects eventually have a way of humbling even the hottest rider. That's why I modify my style according to attitude, desire, and athletic ability of the individual horses I ride.

There have been times I've thrown my hands in the air, wondering what to try next; I've exhausted all my tricks. But I'm strengthened and encouraged when I think of the number of horses I've seen respond to the basic principles explained in this book.

121

11 PROFILE: SHARON CAMARILLO

The Moppet on her first birthday.

Once upon a time, a little blond-haired moppet named Sharon Avril Meffan spent her Saturday mornings on the seashore at Redondo Beach with her father, Bob Meffan. Other children and adults were there, too, swimming, wading, building sand castles with moats. The moppet didn't care for that type of play at the beach, however. She was there because of the ponies that stood tethered behind the crowd.

The man who owned the pony ride attraction was well acquainted with Sharon and her father; every weekend was pretty much the same. Sharon would climb into the saddle eagerly, the pony would begin to walk, and soon she would urge her father to "make him go faster." Bob would oblige by leading the pony into a trot; his daughter's pony rides were cute, he thought, and he enjoyed them very much. The end of each ride was also predictable. Sharon knew she would have to wait for another week for her next ride, and that's when she cried.

Bob would drive the few blocks to their house, a pleasant middle-class home located in a residential neighborhood filled with other young families. Throughout the 1950s, Sharon grew up with nearly everything a child could want—a bicycle and roller skates, "Leave It To Beaver," and "Father Knows Best" on television, and plenty of friends in the neighborhood. Her mother, Avril, was a devoted homemaker and mother, and quite a seamstress, too. Her sewing machine kept Sharon and Sharon's younger brother Kenneth in neat, stylish

clothes for school.

Looking back on her childhood, Sharon feels the only thing she didn't have and felt she really needed, was a horse of her own. She couldn't understand why a horse couldn't live in the back yard, and she offered to get a job to pay for hay. Bob tried to explain to his daughter that she would have had a horse if he could have afforded it, but it wasn't feasible to keep a horse in town anyway.

Bob Meffan was an aeronautical engineer at Nortronics, a firm located in the Los Angeles area. Before marriage and family, he was an adventurer who hitchhiked through South America, traveled the South Seas, climbed mountains, and even worked as a pilot for TACA (Transportes Aereos Central Americanos), freighting cargo into jungle villages. He liked to fly and sky dive; he still loves the outdoors, especially fishing. The entire Meffan family enjoyed camping and fishing together. The experiences instilled in Sharon a love of the outdoors she has never lost.

Their best vacations, as far as Sharon was concerned, were spent in the Sierra Mountains near a pack station. She outgrew ponies, but her interest in horses and riding continued to expand. By the time she was around ten years old, she was certain she wanted to be a forest ranger who owned her own horse.

She frequented an alley behind a Redondo Beach neighborhood grocery store, every day after school. Her mission in the alley was to secure a cardboard box and fill it with carrots that

With family members: Seven the barrel horse, Skeeter the barn cat, and Sugar the spoiled pooch.

The Meffans did a lot of fishing in those days. Here's Sharon with her dad, displaying a nice catch.

The argument may seem trifling today, but at that time, women and girls weren't seen in pants very often, especially in the city. Bob was afraid his daughter was turning into a tomboy; the pony rides had been cute, but Sharon's growing obsession with horses was getting old, very fast.

Mom was a little less concerned about Sharon's choice of clothes. Avril made a variety of western shirts to Sharon's specifications. "We couldn't afford to go out and buy all the western clothes I wanted," Sharon remembers, "so I'd look in magazines and pick out what I liked. She made them, and I wore them; I was always proud when she finished a new shirt for me."

Sharon had more riding opportunities by the time she was a teen-ager. Family friends purchased a livestock commission company, and Bob spent his weekends hauling Sharon to the yards. She and her friend Wendy, whose dad owned the auction, worked horseback, moving cattle through the ring. The horses were also routinely tried on a barrel pattern set up on the grounds.

The turbulent teens were a trying time for the Meffan household. Sharon wanted to spend every Saturday at the auction, rather than join the family on weekend outings in the mountains. Although Bob and Avril are proud of Sharon's accomplishments in rodeo today, Bob was constantly irritated by his

had been discarded by the grocery store. With produce in hand, she walked to a nearby riding stable, and fed a carrot or two to every horse in every pen.

She knew each horse by name, and was able to ride several of them. Occasionally, one of the owners, observing the horse-crazy youngster, would offer to let her ride. Or if that didn't work, Sharon could always strike up a conversation: "That's a nice horse you've got there, mister. . . . "

Only the coldest heart could have said anything but, "Thank you. Would you like to hop on and ride?" When that happened, Sharon's day was complete. Her walk back home was filled with euphoria, and it was only when she entered the house that reality set in once again.

"Sharon, every time I see you, you're in jeans," Bob often scolded. "None of the other girls your age wear jeans. Now go put on something besides boys' jeans!"

"But daddy," she argued, "jeans are what you wear around horses. That's my lifestyle; it's what I want to do."

"Horseback riding is a hobby for you, not a lifestyle," he retorted. "My hobby is sky diving, but you don't see me wearing my parachute around town."

Bob Meffan, the parachute enthusiast.

daughter's single-minded interests in those days. She was definitely not interested in domestic responsibilities, like cleaning the house or doing dishes, jobs that Bob felt should be a natural for every girl. Ironically, years later, Sharon turned out to be an excellent cook and immaculate housekeeper. And Bob and Avril are Sharon's most ardent fans.

It's also ironic to look back and realize the unwitting role Bob played in shaping Sharon's future. In a sense, he was the cause of his own irritation. He was the one who introduced her to the pony rides, and he was the one who got kicked in the stomach, running alongside one of Sharon's rental horses, urging him to lope. It was Bob who took her to the sale yard, and when the fourth National Finals Rodeo came to Los Angeles after being held for three years in Dallas, Bob took his daughter to the rodeo.

Sharon remembers sitting with him in the audience, watching the events. She was dressed in her matching Levi's pants and jacket, and western hat, all items she had saved for with her allowance. She felt a twinge of embarrassment for Bob because he didn't look like a cowboy.

"I loved the rodeo, and I could tell he liked it, too," she says. "The barrel racing was exciting for me. I could just feel that rush of adrenalin. I said to myself, 'Someday I'll be out there, and he's going to watch me, and he's going to be proud of me.'"

She didn't know it at the time, of course, but her future husband, Leo Camarillo and his brother Jerold, were also watching the rodeo. The two boys

had managed to sneak in behind the roping chutes, where they had a ground-level view of the action.

Sharon was graduated from Aviation High School in 1966. Dad wanted her to attend El Camino Junior College, eight miles from home and fairly economical. Sharon had already checked, and realized that El Camino didn't have a rodeo team, but that Pierce College in the San

Sharon and younger brother Kenneth.

She enjoyed riding at pack stations and dude ranches in the Sierras.

With mom, Avril Meffan: "I've always respected my mother for her devotion to family and home."

Fernando Valley did field an intercollegiate team. So she bargained with father, and a compromise was struck. She could attend Pierce, another junior college, and she would take the clerical courses Bob insisted on, along with the agricultural and animal science classes she wanted. Bob and Avril felt college rodeo was a fine activity, but their primary goal was insuring that both children received an education that would give them a comfortable future.

Sharon took a couple horses with her and kept them at a friend's place near school. She used Walter for barrel racing, and Uncle for goat tying. She also continued to stretch family relations when she brought a goat home with her and put him in the back yard. Even Avril, the world's most understanding mom, was dismayed when she opened the back door and saw the goat slip past her, run into the living room, and hop on the couch. Sharon practiced tying the goat, and practiced roping stationary objects on the ground. At the college rodeos, she entered goat tying, breakaway calf roping, and barrel racing. She won the regional college championship in goat tying and all-around categories, and secured a scholarship to prestigious California Polytechnic at San Luis Obispo, a school that has produced a long line of pro rodeo champions.

En route to her 1970 collegiate championship in goat tying, Sharon fell and fractured an arm during a practice session, just days before she was to leave for the College National Finals at Bozeman, Montana. She refused to have a cast on the arm, because that would hinder her in competition. Instead, she talked the doctor into a prescription for pain pills. Mom drove her to the Finals, Sharon won the title, and also finished runner-up for the Miss College Rodeo crown. The latter is a contest based on poise and appearance, as well as horsemanship, so even then Sharon was making good on her goal to combine style with rodeo competition.

When she graduated with a degree in business administration, two thoughts were on her mind—to get a better barrel horse, and to find a job that would be compatible with rodeoing. She wound up buying another horse, and flying with Western Airlines as a flight attendant. The job was ideal for her; she lived with David and Robin Hayes, friends in the Pomona area, and spent a lot of time on the flight reserve list: "I could ride with the telephone outside, and if the airline called me for work, I was within an hour of the airport."

Ideally, she would work Tuesday, Wednesday, and Thursday, which left a long weekend for rodeoing in the WPRA. Whenever a leave of absence was available, Sharon would take it and go on an extended rodeo tour. Whichever horse she was using at the time would invariably begin to work better because she was spending more time with him.

It was during one of those extended leaves from work when she first met Leo. There was a brief, casual conversation, and about six months later Leo invited her on a dinner date. He picked her up, and was dressed in pretty modish clothing. He didn't *look* like a cowboy, and Sharon was visibly taken back.

Her previous dates had been with young men she knew fairly well and liked, and nearly all of them had been cowboy-types. She knew if she ever married, her husband would be a rodeo cowboy, a rancher, or someone in the horse business. But Leo didn't look the way he was supposed to look, to Sharon. They had their first argument that night, but, within a year they were married. The Camarillos will "butt heads," as Sharon calls it. They're both competitors, in and out of the arena. "Any marriage is going to have its ups and downs," she says. "Usually, the reason a marriage lasts is because of love, respect, and admiration. I've always said, the proudest moment of my life was riding into my first National Finals Rodeo next to Leo. We're both happy; I know I'm proud of my accomplishments and proud to be married to one of the best cowboys in the rodeo business. I'm living the life I've always wanted to live, and it's not a case of marrying Leo for his gold buckle, which is what he likes to tell people. Heaven knows, that's minor payment for some of the things we've gone through. I married Leo because he has the same goals in life I have. We don't want to settle for second best. We don't want ever to sit back and think we've done all we can do; there's always something bigger and better on the horizon. But sure, we fight, and usually our fights occur when one of us feels the other is stepping on toes."

The boat-rocking waves on the sea of

Goat tying—Sharon raised her hands for time after completing the tie.
Photo by Jim Fain

A portrait of Sharon during her college rodeo days (left), and at the 1970 NIRA awards presentation, the year she won the collegiate championship in goat tying.
Photo by Jim Fain

127

Sharon as flight stewardess for Western Airlines.

will decide where the trailer will go.

The Camarillos support each other in rodeo, albeit in sometimes roundabout fashion. It's easy for Sharon to get down on roping in general, and one roper in particular, "after hauling three horses all night long, by myself." But after Leo won the first annual World Champion All-Around Timed Event Cowboy contest in early 1985—a grueling two-day event in which cowboys had to compete in calf roping, steer roping, team roping, and steer wrestling—Sharon was the first one on the phone to tell friends and family of Leo's success.

Leo says he "has no time for barrel racing," but it pleases Sharon when she sees him watching her make a run. When Sharon hits a cold streak and isn't winning, Leo will help with "encouraging" words—"you obviously can't ride, your horse is washed up, and you had better go home." Invariably, Sharon will be infuriated, and will urge a winning run from her horse the next day.

Aside from her four NFR qualifications, one of Sharon's finest moments in the arena came in the spring of 1980. For several years, the Copenhagen/Skoal Rodeo Superstars Championship was the biggest financial boon to rodeo contestants. It was an invitational affair—the top 16 money-winners in a handful of Professional Rodeo Cowboys Association events, and the top 16 barrel racers in the WPRA.

It featured an exciting "sudden-death" format. The contestants were randomly paired, one-on-one; the winner of each match advanced to another round of competition—and, of course, half the contestants were retired and sent home after the opening round.

Sharon was nervous, thinking of the $18,500 in prize money at stake in her event. She had hauled her horse, Seven, 1,700 miles from California to Ft. Worth to compete in the Superstars and she had paid a $500 entry fee. The thought of returning home empty-handed was not appealing.

She drew the number one position, which meant she would be first to run at each match. That suited her well—she would make her runs, and let the others try to beat her times. But her opening match was against one of the barrel racers she admired most—1975 world

matrimony, to which Sharon refers, are not necessarily private, nor are they completely lacking in humor. During a practice session at the Camarillo arena, Sharon confronted Leo with a wrongdoing she felt couldn't wait until after the roping. Leo proceded to demonstrate to the others the art of flanking a calf, using Sharon as the calf. She in turn got up from the ground, scrappy and game, and gave Leo a shower of dirt.

There have been arguments over where the big three-horse trailer will travel—to a team roping or a barrel race. Painted on the custom-made rig are the words: "Built Exclusively for Leo Camarillo, Five Times World Champion Cowboy." Leo, on occasion—and strictly to help settle the argument—has asked Sharon to kindly step outside, read whose name is on the trailer, and that

Sharon and Seven at their first National Finals Rodeo—Oklahoma City, December 1979.　　**Photo by Ken Springer**

Sharon rode Seven in a hackamore bit at the Superstars competition.
Photo by Jim Fain

At the Copenhagen/Skoal Rodeo Superstars Championships Sharon won her quarterfinals and semifinals matches against two more tough competitors.

Her last run was the fastest time of the entire Superstars competition.
Photo by Ken Springer

At Phoenix, Ariz.,
in 1985.
Photo by Jim Fain

Sharon and Seven are still a solid, winning team, although they don't travel as extensively as they did during the NFR years.

At Las Vegas, Nev.,
in 1985.
Photo by Jim Fain

131

"I knew there had to be . . . a style of clothing that would appeal to the audience and still be comfortable to wear."

National Finals, 1980.
Photo by Ken Springer

champion Jimmie Gibbs of Valley Mills, Texas. Sharon was elated to emerge the winner, and moved on up to the quarter-finals. The pressure and tension eased up; she had made it past the first round.

Seven continued to work as well as he ever had, and Sharon won her quarter-finals and semi-finals matches against two more tough competitors, Kay Garrison and 1976 world champion Connie Combs. Sharon had worked her way up the ladder to the final round of competition. She would compete against the winner of another exciting match between two of the all-time great barrel horses and racers, 1979 world champion Carol Goostree on Dobre, and 1978 champ Lynn McKenzie on Magnolia Missile. Carol beat Lynn by a mere .02 seconds on two runs. Lynn would win the WPRA title again in 1981.

But at that point, Sharon and Carol were matched in the two-run finals. Sharon said later she may have pressured her horse too much in his turns during the first run. Carol out-ran her by a slim margin. In the second and final run, the last of the Superstars Championships, Sharon eased up and relaxed, and posted the fastest trip of the match. Carol's combined time, however, was just .07 seconds faster than Sharon's. Relieved the competition was over, Sharon cried and hugged Carol, congratulating her on the victory. She had wanted to win first, rather than second, but one thing was certain: Sharon and Seven had more than held their own against the top horses and riders in the nation.

Sharon's interest in fashionable western clothing continued to grow from the days of her childhood. The last sewing assignment she gave to her mother was in preparation for Sharon's first National Finals Rodeo. Avril made all the good-looking shirts Sharon wore that year, and among them was a particularly appealing black satin shirt with a red rose sewn on the lapel. A few months later, similar shirts began showing up in barrel racing circles around the country.

"I never wanted to be a particularly

132

National Finals, 1981. **Photo by Ken Springer**

showy, flashy barrel racer who wore a lot of sequins, or anything like that," she says, "nor did I want to look like a horse show contestant with a fitted equitation suit, but I knew there had to be a happy medium, a style of clothing that would look good horseback, please the audience, and still be functional for the cowgirl."

The shirts Avril made to Sharon's specifications pricked the interest of Sally Von Werlhof, creator of the fashionable Salaminder line of women's clothes. Sally asked Sharon to represent the line for women in rodeo, which

Sharon has done.

One of Sharon's goals is to someday establish her own line of barrel racing clothes, based on versatility as well as style. For example: a three-piece outfit—blouse, skirt, and pants.

"The pants would be wide enough at the bottom so you could wear them over boots, but they would still be narrow enough to be in style with what is fashionable right now. Possibly they would have a pleat, because that look is 'in' (and they are comfortable). An important modification would be side pockets, rather than front pockets, because front pockets gap open when you ride a horse. Then a skirt that you could put on with a blouse. You could pack three matching pieces and actually have several different outfits."

Sharon likes to rodeo with Leo, when their schedules mesh, but it can be an uncertain journey at times. They may both be scheduled to compete at the same rodeo the same day, but if Leo is up in the afternoon and Sharon in the night performance, Leo may find another rodeo to rope at that evening. "It's not a nice feeling to see the rig leave," she admits, "and know I'm going to have to scramble to find a ride for myself and my horse." She envisions the day when Leo will slow down, and the two of them can pick their rodeos together, one at a time. She's not sure that day will ever arrive, but it's nice to think about it.

In ten years of marriage, Sharon and Leo have been on two vacations. They've been on some great promotional

Sharon and Leo with "Leo's dog"—Sugar, above. At right and far right: proof that Sharon is no longer averse to wearing dresses. Photo at right was taken by Anna Robertson for a fashion story; at far right—Jan Spencer photographed Leo and Sharon at the Professional Rodeo Cowboys Association championship awards banquet.

Sharon and Seven have been through a lot together—good times and bad. At Albuquerque, 1982, Seven spooked and ran through a parking lot. He rammed into a car and completely severed the tendons above his left knee. Prompt veterinary attention, and months of nursing the injury, made him sound again.

Chance, meanwhile, shows every sign of developing into a solid, winning horse.

tantly hiked part way up a glacier at the far end of the lake. "About five years passed before I got him to take another vacation," she recalls. "We flew to Mexico in 1983."

Leo's ancestors had come from Mexico, so Sharon figured he would naturally find the trip interesting, and would instinctively know "all the best places to see." Wrong on both counts. It was Leo's first trip to Mexico, and he vowed never to return. He inadvertently drank the local water, and got sick.

Sharon may never get Leo to take another vacation, but in other ways she has helped to make life fuller for them both. She's an animal lover at heart and likes to have a pet around the house. "The only pets Leo had as a boy were cowdogs that were either in the way or biting people, so he wasn't very interested in having a dog," explains Sharon. "I really wanted a dog, but not if Leo was dead set against it."

Sharon continued to work on Leo, and the dog subject culminated in an argument on the way to the airport. Sharon was taking Leo to a plane bound for the Denver rodeo when she gave her best shot with phrases like: "That's my house, too, and I should be able to keep a pet;" and, "You know how much I'd like a dog for company;" and the clincher, "You must not really love me."

Leo phoned late that night, and suggested that Sharon begin looking for a dog.

She picked out a blond Cocker Spaniel puppy and named it Peaches. The dog became part of the family, traveled to rodeos, and was a constant companion around the home arena for several years. Leo would announce to those who came to rope with him that, "This is my dog, and she can go anywhere she wants, so watch out for her." It was a sad Christmas at the Camarillo house in 1979, the year Peaches died. She had followed along to the pasture where Leo and Sharon turned out their horses after arriving home from the National Finals in December. Leo's heeling horse Stick fatally injured Peaches when he inadvertently stepped on her as he was turned loose. Another blond Cocker Spaniel has since taken the place of Peaches. Sugar has also become part of the family, and Sharon admits the dog is

tours with rodeo, like the Presidential Rodeo in Washington, D.C., in 1983, and a Wrangler-sponsored tour of Argentina in 1980, but they've made just two trips that weren't somehow related to rodeo. "I think what it boils down to," Sharon says, "is Leo is not comfortable out of his element. When he goes, there has to be a reason why. Really, his idea of a vacation is to sleep."

A few years after they were married, Sharon planned a bonafide vacation. Leo had a roping school scheduled in Calgary, and Sharon arranged for the two of them to leave a week early, fly to Vancouver, get on a Canadian Pacific train, and go across the Rockies into Banff. They would spend a couple of days at Lake Louise, and catch the train again to Calgary.

To his credit, Leo did agree to join Sharon on the trip. He prowled around the train like a cub bear in a cage, caught up on his sleep at the lodge, and reluc-

"spoiled rotten."

Sharon acquired an antique bird cage on one of her rodeo travels. One of the hobbies she enjoys most is seeking out antique shops in the various towns she travels to, and the cage caught her eye with its vintage styling. No one hangs up an empty bird cage, however, so she bought a parakeet to go with it. Her pet collection is rounded out nicely with a barn cat, named Skeeter.

"Home is important to me whether I'm there or not," she says. "I want my roots—they grow deeper each time I'm home. I also enjoy my little collection of antiques and dolls, a hobby I share with my mother. And lately I've even had time to go fishing with dad."

When things become "too relaxed" around the house, Sharon turns her attention once more to horses and highways. She's ready to go again.

Front entrance, the Camarillo Ranch.

12 RULES

Barrel racing courses vary, and for that reason winning times will vary from one arena to another. That's why no official "record times" can be established for the entire sport.

Rules from Women's Professional Rodeo Association rule book. Check the current WPRA book each year for complete rules, and for any changes that may be made in rules.

MEMBERSHIP

Non-members may purchase from the WPRA one permit a year to contest in WPRA or PRCA approved events for sixty dollars ($60.00) each. This does not include insurance or the WPRA News.

   a. Permit holders are considered apprentice members and may compete in unapproved events, except those held at PRCA rodeos.

   b. A permit holder can purchase 1 permit a year until an accumulative total of $1,000 has been reached. Once she has reached $1,000, she is no longer eligible to retain permit status at approved WPRA events. Money won at approved barrel races where non-members are allowed to compete will count towards filling a permit.

   c. A contestant is eligible to purchase her WPRA card after winning $250.00 on her permit. Money won at any All Women's Rodeo or event sanctioned by WPRA will be accepted.

   d. When a permit holder wins her $1,000 limit before a rodeo is completed, she will be allowed to complete her runs at that rodeo and rodeos previously entered.

BARREL PATTERN

1. Standard courses should be used whenever possible. The standard distances for Barrel Races are:
   a. 90 feet between barrel 1 and 2.
   b. 105 feet between barrel 1 and 3 and between 2 and 3.
   c. 60 feet from barrels 1 and 2 to scoreline. Scoreline should be at least 45 feet from end of arena.
   d. Maximum distance of 105 feet between barrels 1 and 2 and 120 feet between 2 and 3, and 1 and 3. Scoreline must never be more than 90 feet. Above rule is for unusually large arenas.

2. The following shall be used in smaller arenas.
   a. The scoreline should be at least 45 feet away from the end of arena, unless there is a center alley or size does not permit.
   b. Barrels 1 and 2 must be at least 18 feet from the sides of the arena. In

extra small arenas they may be less. In no instance should they be any closer than 15 feet from the sides of the arena.

c. Barrel 3 should be at least 36 feet from the end of the arena, and no closer than 25 feet. In narrow arenas, the 3rd barrel should be set at least 15′ longer than the 1st and 2nd barrel.

d. If arena size permits, barrels must be set 60 feet or farther apart. In small arenas it is recommended the pattern be reduced proportionately to a standard barrel pattern.

Printed with permission of Women's Professional Rodeo Association, Rt. 5, Box 698, Blanchard, Okla. 73010.

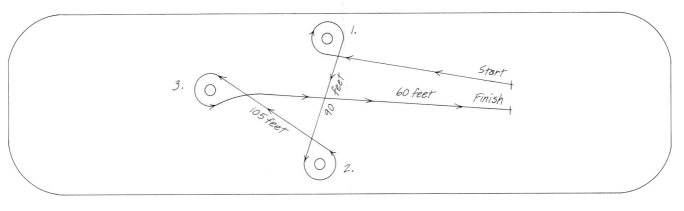

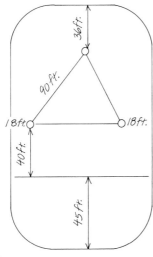

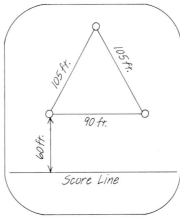

13 TERMINOLOGY

ARC—In this context, arc refers to the flexible "bending" desired in barrel racing horses during a turn around a barrel. The horse's body literally forms a slight curve from nose, through poll, shoulder, and loin as he shows free-flowing movement in front and behind. The inside hock reaches up and across the outside hock in such a turn.

AVERAGE—Competitions with more than one go-round pay prize money for each round, plus money for the best average, or total time. The winner of the average is the overall winner of the contest.

BOWING—Pronounced "bo-ing." This is a problem—rather than completing a proper turn around a barrel, the horse attempts to stride out too quickly, before he's in position to run to the next point. Consequently, a quick turn is sacrificed for a wide, gradual turn. The horse is also out of position for his next turn, and time is lost on the course. This can be caused by the rider rising out of the saddle too soon, before the turn is completed (see Chapter 8).

CHECKING—Refers to the process of "checking up" a horse to get him accustomed to a new bit, to help him limber up, or to make him more responsive to a bit. The process involves tieing rein or reins from head to tail or various parts of the saddle, and is explained fully in Chapter 5.

DEDICATION—Setting aside time for a particular purpose; self-sacrificing devotion.

DIRECT REIN—Another common term for this is "plow reining." If a turn to the right is desired, the right-hand rein will be used to pull the horse's head to the right. The opposite of direct reining is indirect reining.

ELECTRONIC EYE—The automatic timing device used at many professional rodeos. The eye is placed at the start/finish line, and time begins when the contestant and her horse cross a tiny beam of light projected across the arena. Time ends when the beam is crossed again at the conclusion of the run.

ENDURANCE—Ability to withstand hardship, adversity, stress.

ENTRY FEE—The amount of money a contestant pays to enter a competition. Entry fees are pooled to form prize money at jackpots; additional "purse money" is added to the fees for a total prize money at rodeos.

FLAGGER—At rodeos where an electronic eye is not available, one of the judges will serve as a flagger for the barrel race. Standing at the start/finish line, the flagger will drop his flag when the competitor crosses the line at the beginning of the run, then drop the flag again at the completion of the run. Another person with a stopwatch will time the run between flags.

GO-ROUND—Also referred to as "round." A competition will have at least one go-round; a go-round is complete when every contestant has competed once.

INDIRECT REIN—Opposite of direct rein. While the direct rein controls the direction of the front end, the indirect rein controls and stabilizes the outside shoulder and hind leg.

JACKPOT—A competition in which only entry fees are pooled for prize money. No purse money is added.

PATIENCE—Bearing trials calmly; manifesting forbearance under provocation or strain.

Bird's-eye view of the Camarillo Ranch: Sharon with Seven, Leo with Stick.

POCKET—The turning area between horse and barrel. This area varies among individual horses.

POINTS—Where rider looks in a course in order to ride horse in proper directions.

PURSE MONEY—Also referred to as "added money." This is the money added by a rodeo committee. Entry fees plus purse money equal prize money at stake in a rodeo event.

RATE—In barrel racing, rate is the maneuver in which the horse shortens or adjusts his stride in order to turn a barrel.

SHOULDER ELEVATION—Upright position shoulder must remain in to maintain balance in a turn.

SLICING—This is a problem. The horse tries to turn a barrel too soon, and either hits the barrel or turns improperly, out of position to run to the next barrel. The solution is in Chapter 8.

WOMENS PRO RODEO NEWS—Official publication of Women's Professional Rodeo Association. This tabloid newspaper is published monthly, and contains complete information on up-coming WPRA-sanctioned contests, competition results, and other news of interest to members and fans. Address is Rt. 5, Box 698, Blanchard, Okla. 73010.

NOTE ON THE PHOTOGRAPHY

All but a few of the instructional photographs in this volume were made using two Nikon 35mm cameras equipped with motor drive units, and an assortment of lenses.

One of the camera bodies used was a Nikon FM2 and the other was the more electronically elaborate Nikon FE2. The lens that was used the most was the very versatile Zoom-Nikkor 35-105mm, f/3.5.

Another frequently used lens was a Zoom-Nikkor 80-200mm, f/4. With just these two lenses, a wide range of photographs could be taken, from wide-angle shots to telephoto close-ups. The Nikon MD-12 motor drive units on each camera made it possible to capture every detail of Sharon Camarillo's training and riding techniques, even when she was moving quite rapidly. The maximum framing rate with these units is 3.5 frames per second.

Tri-X film was used for the black-and-white photos because of its speed and its ability to record middle tones, even in high contrast lighting. The color photographs on the front and back covers were made on Kodachrome 64. Both are Kodak films.

In order for the photographer to get a clear perspective of the action in the arena, many of the photographs were taken from a scissor-lift platform capable of rising to an elevation of approximately 30 feet. Over 3,000 frames were exposed (approximately 80 36-exposure rolls of film) in order to present the outstanding assortment of instructional photographs in this book.

—*DARRELL ARNOLD*

THANK YOU

To American Hat Company, Houston, Tex.; Jimmy Court
and Gary Parsons of Court's Saddlery, Bryan, Tex.;
Sam Harrington of Sam's Hair Fantastic, Chico, Calif.;
David Hayes, DVM, Meridian, Ida.; Joe Magistri Jr.,
horseshoer, Lodi, Calif.; Ruth Smith, DVM,
Lockeford, Calif.; and Sally Von Werlhof of
Salaminder, Inc., St. Louis, Missouri.

—*SHARON CAMARILLO*

Western Horseman Magazine

Colorado Springs, Colorado

The Western Horseman Magazine, established in 1936, is the world's leading horse publication. For subscription information and a list of other Western Horseman books, contact: Western Horseman Magazine, Box 7980, Colorado Springs, CO 80933-7980; ph. 719-633-5524.